THIS SH*T WORKS

THIS SH*T WORKS

THREE OF THE BEST STRATEGIES TO CREATE CONSISTENT INCOME IN TODAY'S REAL ESTATE MARKET

KENT CLOTHIER

LIONCREST
PUBLISHING

THIS SH*T WORKS
Three of the Best Strategies to Create Consistent
Income in Today's Real Estate Market

ISBN   978-1-5445-1486-4 *Hardcover*
       978-1-5445-1485-7 *Paperback*
       978-1-5445-1484-0 *Ebook*

Dedicated to You

I want you to know that all of your "thank you" cards, all of your emails, all the gift baskets sent to the office tell me we're doing a good job for you, and we appreciate it. I don't want you to think for a second that it goes unnoticed.

We have an entire wall in our office filled with thank-you cards and emails, people sharing with us how much our systems, strategies, trainings, masterminds, and support have changed their lives for the better. And we talk about it every week. We take it very seriously. It means the world to us that you see it and acknowledge it, and that you let us know it matters to you as well.

We're humbled by each and every one of you. We try to be as genuine and authentic as we know how to be; we don't sugarcoat it. I'm not here to blow a bunch of sunshine up your ass.

I'm here to tell you how it really is, but I'm also here to encourage you to get involved and to get going, and not let this opportunity pass you by. We don't ever want you to live a life of regret, where you sit back and say, "Man, I wish I had got involved back in the day." We want you to get involved now, and we'll demonstrate to you how it's done. We will empower you to do it. We will give you the tools and training to make it all happen.

Kent Clothier, president, CEO
Real Estate Worldwide (REWW)

CONTENTS

WHY LISTEN TO KENT?.. 9
WHY THREE BOOKS? 19
WHY YOU WON'T FINISH THIS BOOK 23
INTRODUCTION 25

BOOK ONE: REVERSE WHOLESALING
1. WHAT IS REVERSE WHOLESALING?............................... 33
2. OLD-SCHOOL VS. NEW-SCHOOL WHOLESALING.................. 41
3. 5 KEY STEPS TO CASHING IN WITH CASH BUYERS 47
4. SYSTEMATIZE YOUR BUSINESS 69
5. WORKING YOURSELF OUT OF A JOB AND INTO A BUSINESS.... 77

BOOK TWO: HOW TO PURCHASE REAL ESTATE OUT OF THE AREA
6. BLUEPRINT FOR SUCCESS.. 89
7. HOW TO CHOOSE A GREAT INVESTMENT MARKET............. 103
8. CHOOSING THE RIGHT TEAM.................................... 109
9. CHOOSING THE RIGHT HOUSE 115
10. PAPER RETURNS VS. REAL-LIFE RETURNS 117
11. ALWAYS BUY NEIGHBORHOOD NORMAL 121

BOOK THREE: HOW TO BE A PRIVATE LENDER
12. WHY PRIVATE LENDING?... 125
13. THE INEFFICIENT TRUTH... 133
14. YOUR KEY TEAM MEMBERS 139
15. IMPORTANCE OF DUE DILIGENCE 157
16. WORKING WITH BORROWERS AND LENDERS.................... 185
17. UNDERSTANDING VALUE 201
18. THE STRUCTURE OF A DEAL 213
19. PRACTICES OF THE DEAL.. 225
20. DOCUMENTS AND PAYMENTS..................................... 233
21. LOAN SERVICES, GUARANTEES, AND CAVEATS 241

FINAL THOUGHTS 251
ACKNOWLEDGMENTS 253
ABOUT THE AUTHOR 255

WHY LISTEN TO KENT?

Listen to me not because I've been successful, but because I've been banged around so much over the years and learned so many lessons. My hope is you don't have to go through all the hard lessons I did.

As it stands today, my entire life revolves around time, getting the most out of every minute, and being painfully aware that the clock is ticking on my life. This may sound a little morbid but that doesn't make it any less true. I'm always working to compress time, which I'll explain a little later.

I have dedicated my life to figuring out how to get the best out of life as fast as I can and then sharing that journey with others. Which brings us to how I got to this place. How did I arrive here?

I'm extremely fortunate that my father got me involved in business at the ripe old age of seventeen. I've had the entrepreneurial drive in me since I can't even remember. I started in my father's business, which ultimately became an arbitrage business (that simply means we were trading on the inefficiencies of a market). We were finding products at one heavily discounted price and turning around and selling them in markets where the price wasn't being discounted.

For example, we would buy a truckload of Peter Pan peanut butter for $40,000 in Miami, Florida, and ship it to Omaha, Nebraska where we sold it for $60,000. We did this thousands of times a year.

From the time I was seventeen until the time I was twenty-three, I sat in the front row with my father and helped to build a $50 million-a-year company. At the ripe old age of twenty-three, I was officially put in charge of the company when my father retired. We took it from $50 million to $90 million in the first year. Our company was purchased, and within a few years, I was effectively running an $800-million-dollar sales organization in the grocery business, based out of Boca Raton, Florida. Over the course of the next three years, we turned this $800 million a year company, with a twenty-seven-year-old kid running it, into a $1.8 billion operation and the seventh-largest privately held company in the state of Florida.

Very few people run multimillion-dollar, much less billion-dollar organizations in their twenties. You can imagine from the time I was seventeen to the time I was thirty, all of this success made me a little bit jaded. My world and my perspective were heavily influenced by my experiences. I did not think I could fail at business because I had not failed yet. I thought it was quite natural to be making hundreds and hundreds of thousands of dollars a year, if not millions. I lived an amazing life on the intercostal waterway in Boca Raton and had all the toys, all the cars, all the watches, the big 401(k). You name it, and I had it.

Fast-forward to March 14, 2000. I had a run-in with my business partners, the owners of the company. Because they purchased my company a few years earlier, I no longer had any ownership. I decided to ask for ownership, and when the president and CEO didn't go for it, everything changed. In a matter of minutes, this thirty-year-old punk, who was completely full of shit, made a split-second decision to quit and walk out. It changed the course of my life forever.

I quite literally thought I would just be able to go and start my own business and be back on top in a matter of weeks. Instead, over the course of the next twenty-two months, I proceeded to lose every single thing I'd ever worked for. Every dollar, every relationship, every friend, everything I had ever accomplished in my life—it vanished. It was all my own doing.

To put this poor decision in perspective, I will share the magnitude of what I lost. I had more than $2 million in the bank when I walked out the door. Twenty-two months later I had less than $4,000 to my name. I was like a bad gambler, just chasing it all the way down, thinking I was making the right business choices but continuing to make poor decision after poor decision.

In December of 2002, I saw a late-night infomercial about real estate. The speaker was talking about flipping houses. I'd never heard of such a thing. I had no idea that was even possible. I got a few books, I bought a few courses with money I really didn't have. Yet in a few short weeks I flipped my first house and made $8,000.

One of the biggest lessons I have learned is that if you're going to build a business, you should build a life based on things that matter—because any business is just a few decisions away from being out of business. It could be the economy. It could be business partners. It could be the government. It could be any number of things that can disrupt your business and effectively put you *out* of business. So why not focus on something you're passionate about and put your family first? Figure out how to get the most out of your business, aka control, and own your time instead of being a slave to a business—because in the end, it can be yanked from you in a second. That is lesson number one.

The second story I want to share is about my Uncle John, one of the best mentors in my life. He was somebody I admired very, very much, an executive in the travel business who was well respected in the entire industry. Everybody knew his name. He spent a lot of time with me when I was trying to get back on my feet and rebuild my confidence. When he retired in his early sixties, he had more money than most people could ever even dream of. He had seen the world, but he'd also done a lot of it away from his family.

Shortly after he retired, he was told that he had a form of throat cancer. He began dying in that moment. Here was this great huge man who had a presence, who could control any room in the world, and he was scared. When he heard those words, they scared him.

Just a few months after he was diagnosed, my mother called, telling me my uncle was asking for me because he was about to die. He was in the hospital in Daytona, Florida, so I got in my car in Delray Beach, Florida, and drove as fast as possible to my Uncle John's deathbed. I remember running down the hallway of the hospital and coming into his room. He was hooked up to so many machines, he could barely breathe. He was a shell of himself—almost unrecognizable. He had this little handheld whiteboard that he was using to try to communicate. He wrote, "Celebrate my life," and "I just wish I had more time." Here was a man who could afford to buy just about anything he wanted in the world. He had multiple houses and could afford to go anywhere and do anything. Everything he had worked so hard for in this life couldn't buy him the one thing he wanted the most right then, which was time. His situation had a profound effect on me.

I held his hand. He knew I was there. I could tell by the way his eyes lit up that he was happy I was there. He passed within a few hours. I'm so grateful that I got to spend that time with him because it changed the course of my life forever. In that moment, I realized everything I had ever thought was important—working hard to build businesses, working hard to be recognized, and having authority and power and people's respect—none of it really mattered. The only thing that mattered was time. I knew I had to focus on spending time with my kids, my family, my friends, and making a positive impact on the world.

A few months after the hospital visit with my uncle, I was on a Delta flight from Atlanta to West Palm Beach. My wife and daughter had flown out to surprise me at an event. Now, on the flight home, our different itineraries meant we weren't seated together. I was in 19A while they were in 26E and F.

Midway through the flight, a burnt electrical smell filled my nostrils. I looked up from my laptop to see white smoke billowing down the aisle, which is nothing you ever want to see on an airplane. To make matters worse, the flight attendants freaked out on the overhead speaker.

Here we are, on a plane filled with smoke, alarms now going off and the flight attendants effectively screaming from the speakers. You can imagine the chaos. Your life is flashing in front of your eyes. You conclude you're going to become a statistic. Everybody is screaming, yet the only people I could hear clearly were my wife and daughter. It was such a massive shock to my system that in this one moment, where my little daughter needed me the most, I actually couldn't do anything to help her.

In a matter of seconds, the plane went into a dive. I now know that that was what the pilots are supposed to do, although I didn't then: if they believe the plane is on fire, they go into a dive to try to put out the flames. Well, that's exactly what we did.

Now real panic set in. The masks dropped into mass hysteria. People were freaking out everywhere. The captain came on to explain we were making an emergency landing in Tampa. It was utter chaos, utter panic, and one of the most frightening experiences I've ever had in my life. It was so frightening that I took my phone out and started filming so my son would be able to see what was going on, and then I turned the camera to myself to film goodbye. I wanted to make sure that he knew that in my final moments,

I was actually thinking of him, too. I carry that video with me to this day.

Now, obviously by virtue of me writing this, you know everything worked out. We made an emergency landing in Tampa. The fire trucks came. We all deplaned. Everybody was hugging and crying. The airline wanted us to get back on the plane as soon as maintenance was finished. But you can bet your ass that was never going to happen. I rented a car and we drove to West Palm. On that three-hour drive, I reflected on all that had happened. I was so grateful to be alive.

As a result of these three experiences in a relatively short period of time, I clearly saw that time is not on my side; it could be taken from me in a second. I concluded I needed to focus everything I have on creating freedom and liberating myself from all of the constraints of having to trade dollars for hours. I needed to figure out a way to build a business that not only created active income but also passive income, where my money was making me money; a business that would allow me to spend time the way I wanted to spend it, not the way I had to. I needed to give myself options.

I didn't want to be a slave to the business anymore. I wanted to make sure that I was there for every moment of my little girl's life, and for every moment of my son's life. I wanted to be the ultimate dad, the ultimate husband, and the ultimate leader. I didn't want to be that guy who was phoning it in, like I had been in the grocery industry.

I wrote at the beginning of these pages that I believe in compressing time. What I mean by that is figuring out how to get more out of every day. In other words, most people trade one hour of time for one hour of wages. What the most successful people in the world do is figure out how to be paid in multiple ways. As I sit here today, in this hour, I'm getting paid for what I'm doing inside one business, but other businesses are also bringing in money. In addition, private money is coming in, along with rental income.

When you pick up a book like this, you're trying to figure out how to make more money. I get it. I would argue that time is your only currency. Money is a by-product of it. Most people don't really want the money. What they want is what the money can buy them, which ultimately is time—more moments, more opportunities, and more experiences. The key to being successful in this business, as in any business, is to move away from trading hours for dollars.

When you focus on time and it becomes a driving factor in your life, you'll be shocked at the opportunities that you will be able to create. In other words, when you chase money, money runs. Anybody who has been in sales or fallen behind on their bills knows exactly what I'm talking about. When you're trying desperately to figure out how to get that extra dollar, that extra paycheck, that extra few hundred dollars, it seems like that's the hardest time to get it. When you focus on time, on creating something that matters and giving yourself options, you'll be shocked at how you attract money into those situations.

Money is like water. It is looking for the path of least resistance. It's your job to create as little resistance as possible and give it the opportunity to flow to you. Money never sleeps. It's always flowing, always moving from one opportunity to the next. You have to put yourself in a situation and give it the opportunity to come to you. That's how time is created. That's how the currency of time is traded.

As of this writing, I'm forty-eight years old. I've been in business for thirty-one years. I've built several multimillion-dollar companies. Our house-flipping organization based out of Memphis, Tennessee (Memphis Invest), just celebrated its 5,000th flip. My family is recognized as some of the most successful real estate investors in the industry, across the entire country. I want you to share valuable tools that have come from those thirty-one years of lessons and successes.

WHY THREE BOOKS?

I will set you up with three techniques that will put you in a situation for money to flow directly to you. As long as you are trading hours for dollars, that is not freedom. You have to learn to create passive income. You have to learn to put yourself in a situation where your money is making you money. There are hundreds if not thousands of ways to do that. What I'm sharing in this book is three ways that are proven right now, in our world, that we in my company see happen, and that we are a part of each and every day.

I learned how to build a business the wrong way and I've learned how to build them the right way. The things I'm sharing here are how to set up systems, automation, and strategies in a very intentional way that ultimately not only gives you the income, but also affords you the time.

There's no nobility in building a business that backs you into a corner, so that all you've done is create another job that robs you of the time you should spend doing the things you love.

In the spirit of being very aware of the time that you must spend to consume the information here and put any of these plans in place, I've divided the book into three sections. They are arranged from the most active way of investing in real estate to the most passive.

Book one describes how to create a wholesale machine that produces big checks on autopilot on a regular basis. Of the three techniques, it is the most active.

Book two is about buying rental properties and having a team manage them for you. Our family business, Memphis Invest, is one of the most successful investing companies in the country. We have perfected this method and the management side. We manage more than 5,000 properties for 2,000-plus investors from all over the world. When it comes to creating passive income through rental properties, there's nobody better.

Book three describes the most passive method, putting your money to work making you money by acting as a private lender. The entire real estate industry functions off of private money. Very rarely does it rely on bank loans.

Consequently, many multimillionaires have created their wealth by effectively becoming the bank.

I will walk you through all three of these processes, step-by-step, so you can confidently use one, two, or all three to create your own passive income empire.

The point behind this book, and quite frankly the point behind everything we do, is to connect the dots for people as fast as humanly possible so they don't have to spend thirty years trying to figure out what we have learned. If I can compress thirty years of information into three really valuable resources for you that can move you to the head of the line, we have accomplished our goals.

You can read all three books, or only one or two. It doesn't matter. If you want to take the journey and learn how to go from being an active investor to the most passive investor, we've got you covered. The three books are valuable as a collection and they're equally valuable as individual resources.

WHY YOU WON'T FINISH THIS BOOK

We both know you won't finish reading this book. There's no shame in that. No judgment. I start reading five or six books a month, but I only finish one to three. Some I start reading, which quickly turns into skimming, which leads to a closed book collecting dust on the shelf. I get it.

Here's what I'm going to do so you don't have to read every chapter, every sentence, and every word, but still can gain the knowledge you need to succeed: videos!

At the end of the introduction you will find a link. Once you click the link and create a free account, you will gain access to my short executive summary videos for every chapter in this book. I will review the chapter content with you, highlighting the things I believe you should focus on and those actions you should implement in a very intentional way.

Over the years, we have built a vibrant community at Real Estate Worldwide (REWW) of very successful entrepreneurs and real estate investors. As of this writing, our education company has helped more than 50,000 students. We've helped thousands and thousands to create their own financial freedom. We've learned a lot of lessons through our own experience and we've learned a lot of lessons by helping others.

My hope in providing the information in this book and the videos is that you become a part of our community. We want to connect with you and play an active role in your journey to become successful in real estate and in life.

INTRODUCTION

I'm about to share with you some of the best insights and techniques that I have ever found for building wealth in real estate. In fact, I'm going to share with you some extremely valuable tips and insights that have taken my family and me years to gather, implement, and perfect. These are the same strategies that we used to build our own real estate portfolios and the portfolios of our clients, who come from all over the world.

I'm going to break down some myths of real estate investing, show you how to navigate the "white noise" of information out there, and help you to start making profitable decisions from this day forward. If you're looking for that "easy button" real estate system that makes it magically rain hundred-dollar bills...*wrong guy, wrong book, wrong training.*

I will give it to you straight, share some of the lessons we've learned along the way, and answer all of your questions. I promise, by the time you finish reading you will have an entirely different perspective on what is really possible when you invest smartly in real estate. What I'm going to share with you is what we have discovered by investing our own money in real estate and by managing the real estate investments of all of our clients over the last few years.

If you're like my family and me, you probably have a burning desire to be in the real estate game. You've probably seen more than your fair share of late-night infomercials, read a few books, been to a few seminars, and maybe even signed up for a few of the programs. But you haven't quite got it all figured out.

I got started the same way. My whole family did except my youngest brother, Brett (he actually went to school for this). The rest of us had that same desire to get involved and we set out to get the information and turn it into cash. We were totally mystified and caught up in the idea of buying a house, fixing it up, and quickly flipping it for a nice payday. What you generally don't hear is how much money you can lose along the way! That romanticized version of a "fix and flip" property that we see on TV every weekend is a long way from the reality of finding, fixing, and flipping a house— and making a profit. They make it look really easy, but it's just not.

I can remember 621 Eagle Drive. It was May of 2007 and we were delighted that we were able to buy it for a great price. It needed a lot of work, but we felt strongly that we could get the work done quickly and on budget. We knew that it would sell fast and for a big profit once we were done.

That didn't happen. We made every mistake in the book. We ran over budget and ended up taking a loss when we sold. (For some reason, when I was at that Rehab Training Seminar, I missed the part about losing tens of thousands of dollars.)

We also made a lot of mistakes buying rentals. If you experience a few instances of buying the wrong property, in the wrong area, with the wrong tenants, you'll quickly figure out that there's more to that than meets the eye.

My point is simple: **this is not a game.** It's not a television show, where a rehab gets done in twenty-two minutes between commercials. This is a business. And if you treat it like one and follow a few simple tips, you'll do better than you've ever dreamed.

Your competition will remain stuck using those strategies that don't work: *bleeding big bucks in the process, spending countless hours working on flipping a house, and all to make a few dollars at best.* If you apply what I share with you, you will be light years ahead of them. My approach is going to require a fraction of the time, none of the headaches, and set you up for consistent monthly income.

You know the power of having property that is in your portfolio, going up in value, creating cash flow for you every month, all while any debt on the property is being paid down by the tenant. That's power. We are at a pivotal time right now. The US real estate markets have begun to swing in the other direction and over the next few years, people just like you and I will build massive wealth. It's important to take advantage of the market that we are in, put yourself in the best position to win, and do it over and over again.

By definition, passive income means that it's not active. You don't have to be involved in the transaction on a day-to-day basis, hour-to-hour basis in order for it to be a profitable situation. I am going to lay out three distinct areas involving real estate that are passive situations.

First, I'll walk you through a way to set up a wholesaling operation that, in the long run, can be very passive. It will be active out of the gate, but over time, it will be passive. Second, I will show you how to buy property out of your area in a passive way. A lot of people only want to buy rental property in their backyard because (1) it makes them feel comfortable that the property is down the street, and (2) it makes them feel comfortable that they can do the work themselves. That is no longer a passive investment. Your time is valuable. If you know anything about the real estate in your own backyard, it's not usually the best deal in the country when it comes to rental properties and cash flow properties. If you live on either coast, in all likelihood the best deals are sitting in the middle of America—the "flyover states." That's why I'll show you how to get comfortable creating a passive situation in which you can profit from those scenarios without having to get involved in any kind of day-to-day activity.

Third, I'll walk you through the benefits of being a private lender. This is probably the most exciting thing, because many people simply have no idea that this opportunity even exists. They don't realize that most of the creative real estate transactions that happen in the world today are done by private individuals putting their money to work and helping other investors (some big, some small) get into deals. The main reason for private lending is traditional financing does not address the secondary real estate market.

Once I pull back the curtains, you'll realize there's this massive opportunity to not only loan your money, but to have it completely secured by a piece of property. You can make ten to twelve times the profit you would make by putting it in a bank, and have it completely secured by a piece of property, and if the borrower doesn't pay you, you get the property. It's an amazing opportunity.

I'm excited to share all of this so you'll take away a thorough understanding that passive income generation through real estate is not only real, it's possible.

BOOK ONE

Reverse Wholesaling

CHAPTER 1

WHAT IS REVERSE WHOLESALING?

Reverse wholesaling is probably the single best strategy you can use to earn quick cash with real estate. A lot of people throw around buzzwords and make overblown claims, but reverse wholesaling is the real deal.

Our team has been using this strategy for years, and it works. In fact, back in 2005, we actually coined the phrase "reverse wholesaling." We started by quickly earning money, and then began teaching the strategy to others. We take a lot of pride in the fact that we've been able to show people a simple, strategic way to make money. Now it seems every real estate guru on the planet is out there promoting his or her own reverse wholesaling strategy. As Oscar Wilde wrote, "Imitation is the sincerest form of flattery."

If you pay attention, if you stick with me, I promise you it will be worth your time. Get all the distractions away. Turn off the TV. Get the dog out of the room. Get the kids out of the room. Do everything you have to do, because this is an investment in your education.

WHY DOES IT MATTER TO YOU?

Let's jump into it. Why reverse wholesaling? Why should you want to do this right now? Because cash buyers are taking over the market. That means there has never been a better time than right now. If you're brand new to real estate, I want you to understand that this is not some fad, and it's not rare. Right now, 30 percent to 40 percent of all real estate transactions nationwide take place with people paying cash. Think about how powerful that is. In four out of every ten transactions, somebody is laying down a check for $50,000, $100,000, $250,000, or a million bucks. Whatever the case may be, they're writing big, fat checks.

Breaking News!

People pay cash for investment property!

People do not pay cash for their primary residence!

This is important! People pay cash for investment property. People do not pay cash for their primary residence.

Cash typically is not the way people buy their own home. In almost every case, even with bad credit, most people can get a loan for their primary residence. If you're paying cash, you're an investor. If you're an investor, you're looking for return. If you're looking for return, that means you're putting money out there to get money back, and you want to keep that going, over, and over, and over. This means, as real estate wholesalers, we have the opportunity to sell to these people over, and over, and over again.

Not only are they paying cash, but they're also buying multiple times. They aren't just one-hit wonders.

This is how you build the business. And this is a very exciting time.

WHY IS REVERSE WHOLESALING THE BEST STRATEGY FOR YOUR BUSINESS?

First, if you're just starting out, or if you still work at a full-time job but are trying to figure out a way to get out from under it and build a business, then you need to be very aware of those three words: **revenue-generating activities**. They are all about strategically putting you in a position to win. The more time you spend focused on revenue-generating activities, the more successful you will be, and the faster it will happen.

Next, reverse wholesaling is relationship driven. This means it is long-term focused, rather than transaction driven, which is about quick hits. It allows you to be strategic and selective with your time.

Third, there's no major financial commitment with reverse wholesaling.

Fourth, this business can be done from anywhere. You can do it from your home, or you can open an office location. You can do it remotely. You can do it while you're on vacation. It really doesn't matter.

Finally, it requires no experience in real estate. Isn't that fantastic? You don't need to ever have done a deal. You don't need to know how to figure out what a property is worth. You don't need to know any of that. The market will tell you everything you need to know. That's how you can get away with not having any experience. (Later in the book I'll explain how to read the market.)

WHAT IS IT?

Wholesaling is extremely simple. It is buying real estate at a deep discount and immediately selling to another investor. You don't try to sell it on the retail market; you don't try to fix it up; and you don't invest a lot of money. You simply buy it and sell it. You don't ever touch it. You flip that contract to another buyer to increase their investment portfolio. That's all wholesaling is. Buy it really cheap and sell it really cheap. You don't try to get retail prices.

DOES THIS WORK?

I got started buying and selling houses back in 2003 in South Florida. My father was flipping houses in Memphis, Tennessee, at the time. And my brother, Chris, began doing it in Denver, Colorado. Yet none of us were working together.

I started 1-800-SELL-NOW down in Florida a couple of years later, to get sellers ringing my phone. And ring they did! Then we tried to become more efficient and bring our buyers into one location. We chose Memphis because my family and friends were there, and we already had a powerful network in place. It wasn't because Memphis was a great market; it was because we had resources we could tap into. By 2007, our business had developed to a point where we needed to make some changes. We started Memphis Invest as a full-on real estate company that bought and sold houses at a much grander scale. In addition to wholesaling, we started adding more services—these took off, and the business boomed.

Then came 2008, the market crashed, and the banks retreated. They stopped loaning money to investors, and this nearly crippled us. To remain in business, we had to make more changes. That's when we started working almost exclusively with cash buyers. We automated the entire system and were pretty savvy about it. Now we can look into a database and see who is paying cash, anywhere in the country, in a matter of seconds. Once we figured that out, we made it available to the public and started selling the service on the real estate market.

That's how we got into the online education and information business. Between the 1-800 numbers and the websites we'd developed, people wanted to do what we were doing. We quickly automated the way we raise private money and brought that system out in 2010. We call that "Find Private Lenders Now."

Today, Memphis Invest has sold thousands of properties, and that number is growing like wildfire. The vast majority of our buyers are from out of state, only a fraction have never been to the state, and almost all of them have referred a friend to us.

Do you think we might be doing something right?

Consider what you just read: we get buyers from other areas to invest with us in sleepy, little Memphis, Tennessee. A quarter of our buyers have never been here, yet almost all of them refer their friends, family, and colleagues to us. We've discovered something, and the key for you is to learn from it.

We recently moved into the Dallas, Houston, Little Rock, and Oklahoma City markets. I don't care whether you're trying to do one, or ten, or twenty, or one hundred, or 500 transactions. I promise you, we can teach you something worthwhile.

HOW DO WE DO IT?

We are extremely focused on our clients. As I said, it's a client-based business, not a transaction-based business. **We focus 80 percent of our efforts on building relationships with buyers.** Everything you've ever heard before is, "Go find a deal. Get a deal under contract, and then you can go flip it to anybody." We won't say that is untrue. But we will tell you this: if you're trying to build a business in which you have little experience or involvement, and you want to build it in a sensible way with little or no risk, then focus 80 percent of your efforts and revenue-producing activities on finding and building a relationship with buyers.

We target and automate our market to buyers and sellers. We do what we call "shopping versus selling." This means shopping for what buyers want versus selling them what we have. Then we tie all the compensation around us to client satisfaction. Everybody that's part of our team, they're just performing for the clients.

CHAPTER 2

OLD-SCHOOL VS. NEW-SCHOOL WHOLESALING

Let's talk about what I mean by "performing for the clients." There are a million different ways to find a great deal. But the point is that the old way began with finding a deal, making a crazy, ridiculously low offer, and hoping it got accepted.

Step two of the old way was to start marketing the deal to the client. But let's be honest here. That person is not really a client. A client is someone whose needs you serve. In the old way, you find somebody out there to buy your stuff. You aren't trying to serve their needs. You don't care if you are helping them. You're just trying to find somebody to buy the property. That's transactional.

Many of you have some experience with this. I know you've gone out there and used classified ads, posted on Craigslist, talked about it on Facebook, and highlighted it on every single real estate marketing site. You go to the local media meeting and you put up bandit signs around the neighborhood, looking for buyers. You hand out fliers. You do everything possible to get it sold. And while you are doing all of this, you realize it is unbelievably nerve wracking. You have all kinds of crazy pressure on you, to the point where you're having sleepless nights and butterflies in your stomach. You're going crazy trying to figure out how you will sell the thing and get to that payday.

Old School Wholesaling

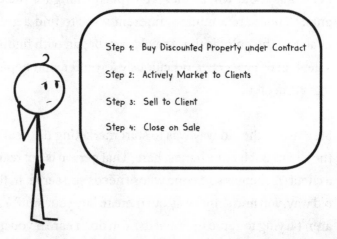

Step 1: Buy Discounted Property under Contract

Step 2: Actively Market to Clients

Step 3: Sell to Client

Step 4: Close on Sale

In some cases, you do sell it. That's when you get to move to step three. You meet with the title company, or the closing attorney or agent, close the deal and get paid.

Yes, you can do that. It does work. Absolutely. But it's stressful and risky, and that's not what you're here to learn. You're here to learn about reverse wholesaling.

NEW "REVERSE" WHOLESALING

Reverse wholesaling is a pretty basic concept. It all starts with the buyer. We get out there and market to cash buyers. We go find **active cash buyers.**

We find active cash buyers who are in the market and already buying. We market to them, asking them to pick up their phone and call us. When they do, we interview them. Our goal is to build a rapport and a relationship. Remember, 80 percent of our efforts go right into building a relationship.

We're just people hanging out with other people who happen to have cash and want to buy real estate. We're just getting to know them. Once we understand who they are and what they're all about, we start identifying what properties they want to buy.

Remember, cash buyers are investors. They always want to buy more. Always. We start figuring out, through a series of questions, exactly what they want to continue to buy.

Once we understand what they want to buy, only then do

we go shopping. That's the reverse part: **start with the client, then go after the property.**

New "Reverse" Wholesaling

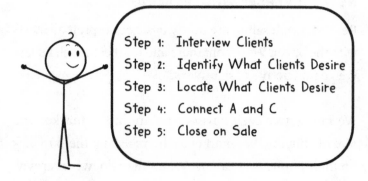

Step 1: Interview Clients
Step 2: Identify What Clients Desire
Step 3: Locate What Clients Desire
Step 4: Connect A and C
Step 5: Close on Sale

Now it's time to shop! We grab our shopping cart, and we start walking down the aisle and finding the items they want. They've told us they want a particular type of house, and a certain type of neighborhood, with a specific return on investment. They've told us exactly what's important to them, whether it's schools, security, rental income, or a no-hassle, no-repairs property. We go out and locate it for them. Once we do, we put it on the contract, turn around, and flip it right back to our cash buyer. It's nice and easy. Everybody gets paid. We close on the deal, and we move on.

This is how we do it.

Think about the old way: putting a property on the contract and crossing your fingers that you found the right kind of property, in the right neighborhood, and at the right price. You are hoping, because you don't have it sold. You just have to hope you run into somebody that wants what you have to offer.

However, using our reverse wholesaling system, you have already talked to the buyers, so you know this is what they want. You don't have to hope. You **know.** They've told you exactly what they want to pay. Therefore, you can quickly back into what you are willing to offer to the sellers you find. That is how "no experience necessary" comes into play. If you know your cash buyers are willing to pay $110,000, and you know you want to make a $10,000 wholesale fee, then you absolutely know the most you can pay for the property is $100,000.

That's just simple math. Without ever looking at a house, if it doesn't fit your budget and your buyers' needs, then you won't move on it, period. If it sounds like we're working backwards, that's partly true. We're starting with the end in mind. Building our relationship with the cash buyer is the entire point. Once we have developed that relationship, we're simply going to go shopping for what they want. This is a very effective strategy, and it all starts with the relationship.

CHAPTER 3

5 KEY STEPS TO CASHING IN WITH CASH BUYERS

We are huge proponents of cash buyers, because they are no-hassle buyers. They make life easy. When we're dealing with cash buyers, we don't have any of the normal problems we encounter in other real estate transactions. Why? **Because there are no banks involved.**

There's nobody between my buyer and me to screw up my payday. There's nobody to make it complicated. The investors are paying with cash, which means they close quickly. Moreover, they want multiples, and this means we can sell to them again, and again, and again.

5 Key Steps to Cashing in with Cash Buyers

Step 1:   Find Active Cash Buyers

Step 2:   Target and Automate Your Marketing

Step 3:   Build Relationships with Buyers

Step 4:   Find Properties for Buyers

Step 5:   Close Deals...Cash Checks

Most people don't fully understand this. If the only house you've ever purchased is your own home, then you probably don't fully understand how banks and loan officers interfere in a real estate transaction. But when there are no banks involved and it's just cash, you can close on a deal (buy it, sell it, and get paid) in less than twenty-four hours. It can certainly happen within seven days.

I know that seems crazy. It's almost like buying a car. You write a check, you exchange the title, and boom! The car is sold. That is almost exactly how it is for a property transaction when a loan officer is not involved. As long as you exchange a clean and conveyable title, nobody cares. Nobody needs to wait. Here's the money; let's go!

What makes it complicated are the banks. If you're looking to get paid within the next seven days on a deal, then you need a cash buyer.

Find active cash buyers. Target and automate your marketing to them. Build the relationship with the buyer. Go find the properties, and then close on the deals.

Now, I'm not here to advertise for FindCashBuyersNow. com. But I will show you exactly how we find cash buyers, fast.

STEP ONE: FIND ACTIVE CASH BUYERS

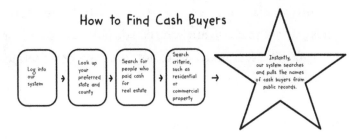

How to Find Cash Buyers

(Pay attention to that last section: these data come from public records.)

When you buy a house or property, that purchase is

recorded and becomes a public record. When that happens, the software we developed (which has taken the industry by storm over the last few years) can pull your name out for us to look at. We can find every single cash buyer in the country, instantly. There's no need for you to spend a lot of time hunting for people paying cash, or for the best buyers in the market. We've automated that for you. It returns this information to you in a flash. You can see every buyer who paid cash is listed. You can see that there are thousands and thousands of buyers just in that one county. You can also see a lot of other information, too. You can view the property they purchased, the zip code where that property is located, how many properties they've purchased that meet your search criteria, the buyer's phone number and mailing address, the date of purchase, and the sales price. It is all in there.

The software is extremely user-friendly. To be perfectly honest, if we can use it, anybody can do it. It's designed for us because, quite frankly, we're not that computer literate. We just need it to work.

The next step is the reason reverse wholesaling works, and it lets you stay in control. Now that you have found buyers, you automate your marketing to them. What we want is for buyers to call *us*. Cold calling is usually what freaks new investors out. They say, "Oh, my gosh! I can't call a buyer! I don't know what the heck I'm talking about, right? I'm brand new to the business. I don't have any experience yet." That kind of reaction is very common.

The solution is marketing materials that position you as somebody worth talking to and who can help a cash buyer. That understanding can make the cash buyer pick up the phone and call you. If buyers call you, the dynamic is different. If you call them, you come off as someone who needs their business. On the other hand, if they call you, they need you. They are responding to your marketing because you have something they want.

STEP TWO: TARGET AND AUTOMATE YOUR MARKETING

So that is the next step: target and automate your marketing. You need marketing pieces that position you as the market leader and the go-to company. You have to be very strategic about it and use very powerful language. Inside of our system, we've already done this. If you have or developed your own system, that's great. Do not spend a lot of time, effort, and energy trying to reinvent the wheel. If it's already been done for you, take advantage of that and use it.

I can't even tell you how much we spent developing these marketing letters. We probably spent over $1 million through the years testing different concepts to perfect this particular marketing communication. We finally got one that works flawlessly every single time. It is effective and the language is very powerful. We call it our "challenge" letter.

With our system, we make it simple for you. All you have to do is plug in your logo, your basic information, and your signature. Again, we're not trying to do a commercial. We just want to talk about the big-picture stuff.

Our system generates letters for you instantly. That's the kind of automation you want. If you're going to sit down and hand type every single letter to every single cash buyer individually, then you're doing it wrong. That is not a revenue-generating activity. That kind of activity simply drains the life out of you, especially when there are systems in place where you can have it done for you for $149 a month. Don't waste your time doing it; make sure processes like these are automated. Send this off to a mail house to do it. Again, that's all built into our systems. If you're using some other system, please make sure that this functionality is built into those systems.

STEP THREE: BUILD RELATIONSHIPS WITH CASH BUYERS

In order to build relationships, you have to know exactly what questions to ask. You need to instill **credibility, trust, and desire** in your buyers. Those are three very important areas that you must address with your clients. Take it from someone who's done this for a long time. If you generate those three feelings—credibility, trust, and desire—you have hit the triggers you must.

How do you do that? First, you have to use objection scripts. This means you must understand what a buyer's potential objections might be, and have well-crafted responses ready.

Build Relationship with CASH BUYERS

- Know what questions to ask
- Create credibility, trust and desire from your buyers
- Question-based selling technique
- Determine your Hot Zone

In most cases you will hear very few objections because, again, they're calling you. If you call them, they'll have all kinds of objections, because you're calling them as a solicitor.

Consider how you feel when somebody cold calls you when you're sitting down eating dinner with your family. You get a call from a phone solicitor and you're ready to throw the phone across the room. You are not ready to do business.

You don't want to be the hunter—the guy making the cold call. You want to be hunted. Again, the well-designed marketing piece makes that happen.

When you finally get on the phone with a potential client, understand that there might be some objections. Anticipate them before the call. For example, a buyer might ask, "Why should I do business with you rather than somebody else?" Have a good answer ready. More importantly, you need to have a series of questions prepared.

This kind of business requires having a conversation with somebody. Think about it: if you want to go shopping for the kind of properties a buyer will want to buy from you, what kind of information do you need? Start from there. Talk to the cash buyer and ask questions. Use your common sense.

Your task is to understand their objectives and what they are willing to buy.

However, don't get caught up in thinking you know more than you do. You don't know half of what you think you know. I say that at the risk of offending you. Consider it a friendly reminder from one of the biggest real estate wholesalers in the country. Anytime you put a box around yourself and say, "Well, I know people only buy in this area," or "I know they only buy in that area," you effectively are closing yourself off to other opportunities.

Remind yourself that you don't know what you think you know. Be open to talking to buyers. Let them tell you what they want to do, what they want to buy, where they want to buy, and how much of it that they want to buy. When you get the answers to those questions, you're building a shopping list that makes you very effective and very strategic as a wholesaler. They'll tell you exactly what they want, and exactly how to sell it to them. How great is that?

As I said before, it's not just about the house or the property. You must understand that this business is 80 percent about building credibility, trust, and desire. You must learn why they are buying. What is it they're trying to accomplish? Knowing the answers helps you sell to them.

STEP FOUR: FINDING PROPERTIES FOR BUYERS

The hot zone is where you, as a real estate wholesaler, get the biggest bang for your buck. It is the zip code, the region, the part of the county where you can invest your time, your effort, and your energy to generate deals and find houses. It is where you are going to invest your time to get the biggest return on investment. In other words, if you spend all your time focused on finding zip code 11111, is that where your cash buyers want to buy? Is that where other cash buyers are buying? How many deals are being sold in that area? How many properties are being flipped in that area? If you get something on the contract, will you be able to sell it?

If you don't know the answer to those questions, then you have no business looking in that area, investing your time, money, blood, sweat, and tears in that area. Why would you ever invest time and money to generate a deal in a zip code that you don't already have presold, or that you at least know you have a good chance of selling?

Focus on revenue-generating activities, always. Move with a purpose.

You need to do a little bit of market research first, before you aimlessly market your properties throughout the entire county. If you start marketing in three, four, maybe five of the hottest zip codes—the hot zones in that county—you're targeting your market, specifically.

Think about a McDonalds or Subway franchise. What did they do before they opened up a successful franchise? They did research! They determined the high-traffic areas, the demographics of the customers, and the building and zoning requirements of a particular location. They did all that research first, so they knew their area would be the most successful spot for their franchise.

Your business is no different. Your product is houses. Your customers are cash buyers, so put your product where the customers are. That's exactly what you're doing by identifying hot zones.

How do we do that? There are a lot of different ways. Once

you have a list of all the cash real estate transactions in your area, you sort them by zip code. On our system, you simply click a little button and all those 11,000 buyers and their transactions are sorted in numerical order by zip code. In a matter of minutes, you can determine that 80 percent of the deals being done are in these five zip codes: those are the hot zones.

We spend money on marketing, but only where we know our cash buyers want to buy, or in the zip codes where we know all the cash buyers are already buying. That's being strategic. That's being smart. That's how you get a huge return on investment. You don't need to be an experienced real estate investor, and you can still outsmart, outwit, and out-negotiate everybody, because you have so much information and you're being so strategic.

I guarantee that if there are one hundred real estate investors in your market right now, not one of them knows what I just explained. You absolutely can be ahead of the game. That is a distinct competitive advantage, because while they're out there spending $5,000 to blanket their county generating a deal, you might spend $500 to advertise in only one zip code and generate a couple of deals from that effort. While they're spending themselves to death, you're leveraging information and getting a much bigger bang for your buck because you've taken the time to do a little market research up front. Focus all your efforts on the hot zones.

Properties from Multiple Sources

- Direct Seller Marketing – Direct Mail, Bandit Signs
- MLS – Realtor Referrals
- Bank REOs
- Probates
- HUD Homestore
- Wholesalers

The figure above lists several sources where you can find properties you can buy, and then sell to cash buyers. Let's look at them in more detail.

Direct Seller Marketing: We know it might be getting repetitive, but in direct seller marketing where you're trying to reach motivated sellers, you can use direct mail campaigns, or bandit signs, or any technique you like. However, the only place you'll target your direct mail campaign or hang that bandit sign is in the exact zip code where you already know buyers are buying, or where the cash buyer you have a relationship with wants to buy.

Multiple Listing Service: When you understand where your hot zone is, you can use the Multiple Listing Service (MLS), (or you have one of your realtor friends use MLS), and set up an alert that breaks down the exact property you're looking for. For example, you know you're looking for property in zip code 11111, and you know your buyer wants to pay $110,000. You also know they want a three-bedroom, two-bathroom house, with a two-car garage, etc. You set up the alert in MLS for that exact scenario. Therefore, you're not hunting and pecking every day. When that property comes up in MLS, you're the very first one to see it, and you immediately make an offer on it.

Bank REOs: If you can develop a relationship with the banks and buy foreclosed properties directly from the banks—that can be one of your biggest sources of properties.

Probates: Probates occur when someone passes away and the estate is tied up in probate court. Typically, the trustee of the estate wants to get rid of a property very quickly, and you can benefit from this by working directly with probate attorneys. You can often find great deals that way.

Even if you have zero experience, but you build a relationship with cash buyers and get those cash buyers very excited, I promise you can earn a bundle. Imagine for a second that you've built a relationship with the cash buyer. They call you and say, "I'm interested. I have your letter here, and I want to spend $300,000 on investment properties in the next ninety days. I've got the cash. It's sitting in a self-directed IRA right now, and I'm ready to make a move."

Think about that. It means you are now a cash buyer. You can go to market and say, "I have cash. I'm ready to spend. I need to get properties in the next ninety days." You can now advertise yourself as a cash buyer because you have this person behind you. By doing that, other wholesalers, other realtors, everybody in your market will start bringing you deals. It's very simple: you simply relay to them exactly what your cash buyers told you they're looking for.

If you have a 1-800-SELL-NOW website, that's another great resource for bringing in deals. In our own business we use REO. A lot of people bring us deals, including other investors and bank REOs. We ALSO get our properties from 1-800-SELL-NOW, direct mail, PPC, banks, HUD, and the Multiple Listing Service.

Understand this: what I am describing is purely a numbers game. We fail 90 percent of the time. In order for us to do nine flips in Memphis Invest every single month, we must create eighteen opportunities each month. Be prepared to make twenty offers to get one deal done. You might do better, and you might do worse. The point is you have to be in the game. You have to make offers on deals in order to get them done. If you made one offer, it wasn't accepted, and you threw your hands in the air and said, "This doesn't work," then you've just determined your fate. You have to make offers over, and over, and over again. Certainly, you are well ahead of the game. You're going shopping for what a cash buyer wants. You understand exactly where to make the offer. You can be more strategic about your offers, but still you must make a lot of them.

STEP FIVE: CLOSE DEALS...CASH CHECKS

The contracts are pretty straightforward. You know your cash buyer will pay $110,000 because they know they'll get $1,500 a month in rent in zip code 11111 for a three-bedroom, two-bath house. As a wholesaler, you're writing offers all day until somebody accepts. Then you find a matching property that you're able to get on the contract for $100,000; this is your purchase contract. Suddenly, you have $10,000 on the line; that's your wholesale fee.

Now what?

First, you write a sales contract for $100,000. By default, every contract ever written is assignable, unless it is otherwise clearly stated in the contract. This means you can transfer your interest in the contract to someone else. I'm not an attorney, and you probably aren't either, so I will make this as simple as possible. You can assign your interest in the contract by specifically writing that into the contract. For example, when I write my name in there, I would say, "I am the buyer, Kent Clothier, and/or assigns."

The phrase "and/or assigns" basically means the contract

applies to me, or whomever I assign it to, or whomever I decide to add to the contract. In the state of Florida, it's literally a checkbox on a standard real estate contract, which you simply check to indicate that you have the ability to assign or transfer it to someone else.

If you don't want to assign a contract, you can do what's called a double close. You write a purchase contract for $100,000. On the contract, you indicate that one condition of the contract is that it must be subject to a fourteen-day right of inspection: anytime within the first fourteen days, you can inspect the property and change your mind. An inspection simply means you can drive up, look at the property, and decide that you don't want it after all. That's all you have to do. For any reason, if you decide that you're not happy about it within the first fourteen days of the contract date, then you can cancel the contract without penalty.

You lose no money. But on day fifteen, your $500 escrow deposit "goes hard." In other words, it's real now. It's legit. You put $500 down. If you decide to cancel within fourteen days, you don't lose $500. On day fifteen, your deposit belongs to the seller.

Now, at the same time you write the contract, you turn around and call your cash buyer, and you say, "Joe, I've got the property you've been looking for. I'm sending over an agreement. I will sell the property to you for $110,000. You have a seven-day right to inspect."

Why do we follow this process? Because if he looks at it inside the seven days and tries to cancel, it still gives me seven days to get it resolved. If he likes it, Joe puts down a $2,500 escrow deposit on his contract. At the closing, the seller and I do our deal, and Joe and I do our separate deal, all in one shot. That is what is called a "double closing," also called a back-to-back closing, double escrow, or simultaneous closing.

We do our deals in Florida because state law there allows us to do what's called an "assignment contract." We don't even fill out a sales contract to Joe. We just fill out a one-page contract that says, "I'm assigning my interest and my buyer contract to Joe for $10,000. You can pay me a fee." That's it.

Once we have contracts in hand (either the purchase and sales contracts, or the purchase and assignment), we take them and the two escrow checks to our title agent or our closing attorney. We set up a closing date, everybody performs an inspection, etc. After the seventh day, our buyer's contract or buyer's escrow money is now mine. After day fourteen, the escrow money we put in play, the $500, is now the seller's.

Here's how the numbers work. I purchased it for $100,000

and my buyer bought it from me for $110,000. We go to the closing table and pick up $10,000, while the other $100,000 goes to the original seller. We bring no money of our own to the table. My potential profit is $10,000. I have a few miscellaneous, negligible costs in there. (Who pays closing costs and does the title search is negotiable.)

Make sure that your title company or your closing attorney is familiar with double closings and how to do them. If they tell you they don't know how to do it, or if they tell you it's illegal, find another closing attorney or title agent. They have no idea what they're talking about.

How Does the Deal Work?

Deal Structure		
Sales Price	$	110, 000
Purchase Price	$	100, 000
Potential Profit	$	10, 000
Your Escrow Deposit	$	500
Buyer's Escrow Deposit	$	2, 500
Profit If Default	$	2, 000

*If your cash buyer defaults and does not close, forcing you to not close with your seller, you lose your $500 BUT your buyer loses their $2, 500 to you – you make $ 2, 000

ESCROW

Let's talk about the escrow, because that can freak people out. I put $500 down with a fourteen-day right of inspection. On day fifteen, it goes "hard," which means the money is in play—it is now nonrefundable, regardless of what happens to the transaction. The buyer, who wanted to buy the property from us, put $2,500 escrow money down, and he had a seven-day right of inspection. On the eighth day, his money goes "hard." On day nine, the buyer picks up his phone and says, "Man, I don't want the deal. I'm out. I'm backing away."

That's fine, because I have his $2,500 sitting at my title company, and it's now mine. I have to call up the seller and say, "Look, I'm sorry, but I'm not going to close."

They're going to tell me, "Well, you just lost your $500 deposit." I'm okay with it. Yes, I lost my $500, but I kept the buyer's $2,500. So, even when I lose, I win. I made $2,000, even though both transactions fell through.

That is why you always require more escrow money from your buyer than you give out to your seller. Even if it goes south, you're still paid for your time. These are **revenue-generating activities.**

You definitely want a closing attorney or a title agent involved with you in every one of your deals. You send them the contracts and let them do all the other legwork. You do not need to know everything there is to know about a contract, or everything there is to know about rehab or repairs. However, the more knowledge you have, the better educated and more effective you will be, which will only make you more money down the road. But at the core, do you need to know all that? No.

What I've shown you is what you need to know. You can bring in professionals to help with the rest of it: title agents, closing attorneys, and mentors.

We use this process every day, and it is beautiful. It's A to B, and B to C, C to D. Done. Boom. That is how you get paid quickly. In the next chapter, I'll discuss your career and life growth—how you turn your job into a real business. I want you to go through the evolution of actually building a business, not just building a job that you own.

CHAPTER 4

SYSTEMATIZE YOUR BUSINESS

If you have never read the book *The E-Myth* by Michael Gerber, I invite you to do that, because it's so powerful. The "E" in the title stands for "entrepreneur," and it discusses the evolution that people go through as they build their businesses. Gerber explains how almost 99 percent of (so-called) small businesses are nothing more than people owning a job.

How do you make that move from owning a job into true entrepreneurship? In our investment company, dealing with buyers from all over the country, we realized we were doing a poor job of taking care of our customers. We were bringing buyers in from California or elsewhere, and they bought properties in Memphis, but they didn't know what to do with the properties once they bought them. They didn't have the resources to rehab them. They didn't have the resources to find and screen tenants or handle maintenance and property management. There was an opportunity for us.

My father and my two brothers are smart business guys, and they realized that if we could provide those services at Memphis Invest, that would be a valuable service to our customers, provide us another income stream, and help our customers to buy more properties from us, more often.

So that's what we did. We started evolving into a complete, turnkey operation. Now we not only acquire and sell properties, we also rehab and manage properties. We do property maintenance, tenant screening, and everything else connected to managing income properties, with one goal in mind: if we can help grease the gears and make buying from us easier for our investors, they'll turn around and buy more from us.

Cash buyers want to buy a lot of properties; give them a reason to buy them from YOU. It's actually very easy to give them a reason. Just do a good job. Take care of them. Focus on the client, not on the deal. Once you've switched to a client-based model instead of a transaction-based model, everything changes. Everything you do revolves around making the customer experience exceptional. Get everybody in your organization focused on the same goal. Many of you are the entirety of your organization. But there are people all around you who can help you. Maybe your realtor. Maybe a property manager. You might introduce your buyer to a friend who's a contractor. You might introduce him to your title agent. Whoever it is, make sure that everybody understands what your vision is, and how you want to tie everybody together toward making it easier for your customer to say yes. In a scenario like that, everybody wins.

Systematize Your Business

Step 1: Close on Sale

Step 2: Begin Rehab Process

Step 3: Close on Rehab in 14 Days, Rental Agents Contacted

Step 4: Rental Agent–Rent Property in 14 Days

Step 5: Close on Tenant

Here's the way our system works. I'm giving this to you because I want to excite your imagination, not because I think you can go off and do this on day one. I want you to see how we evolved into who we are, and how you can start to lay the groundwork to do the same with your own business.

I'm going to walk you through the evolution of this business because how we do business today is different than what we did just a few years ago. What we did many years ago was this:

Imagine that we've just sold you a Tennessee property and you're living in California. You have no idea how to get that house rent ready. You've paid us $50,000, but it requires another $10,000 in improvements so that you can make money on your investment. That is the opportunity that I outlined before. Back then, we stepped in and screened the rehabbers, screened the general contractors, and took on the task of managing that entire process for you. We were able to do in a few weeks what would have taken you months to do.

We realized that our ability to do this effectively was a huge win for our clients. By controlling multiple projects at once, we were able to drive costs down and exert leverage on contractors that an individual buyer could never have done. We began to communicate with rental agents for help renting our properties. We knew the timeline and when the property would be completed. This also created efficiencies for our buyers. They had somebody who was in their corner, a real partner who was able to get a property rehabbed and rented faster than they ever could have.

Our property management company could begin screening the tenants, doing all the due diligence, running background checks, doing credit checks, and getting everything ready for a move-in. All of this moved much more efficiently than if somebody sitting 3,000 miles away were trying to do it themselves.

Today, we have brought all of these services in-house. We own the property management company. We own the rental agents. We own the project managers. We buy property, rehab a property, and then sell it because we've become so good at this entire process—but that was never what we intended doing. What we do now helps us achieve what we always wanted to achieve: it makes the customer experience so good that they want to come back and buy over, and over, and over again. If you take care of them, I can guarantee you they'll come back.

TIE THE TEAM TO THE DEALS

How do you gear up your entire organization to focus on taking care of the customer? To make everybody a part of the deal, you want everybody to get paid out of the deal.

Tie the Team to the Deals

Position	Compensation/Incentive
Buyer's Rep	$1,000
Sales Referral (Potential)	$1,000
Buyer Referral (Potential)	$1,000
Project Manager	10% of Rehab Costs. Bonus $500 if Project is Completed in 14 Days.
Rental Agent	Half The First Month's Rent. Bonus $500 if within 30 days.
Office Bonus	$500 per deal – paid if we hit the monthly goal preset.

In an effort to create this passive income stream, you will have to surround yourself with a team. You will need a leads manager, an acquisitions person, and a dispositions person at a minimum. Eventually you will also need a transaction coordinator.

If you create a $10,000 wholesale fee, your costs would break down something like this. First, you spend 20 percent to 25 percent of that on marketing, or effectively $2,500 for this example. You would also pay an additional 10 percent of revenue to your acquisitions person, or $1,000, and another 10 percent to your dispositions person, another $1,000. At this point you've spent $4,500 from your $10,000.

You have salaried clerical staff whom you incentivize to do more closings. You pay them an hourly wage of somewhere between $15 and $20 an hour, depending on where you are, and probably $250 to $500 per closing. The lead manager would get paid the exact same way a transaction coordinator would: an hourly rate plus a fee for every closing. You're going to have a rough margin here of 45 to 50 percent profit to you, while everybody else is running the deals. The numbers can go up, the numbers can go down, but that's the basic structure.

At this point, everybody's getting paid out of the deal. Everybody is highly incentivized to do more deals. If you wanted to, and we have done this, incentivize your team to reach sales objectives, meaning that if they do ten deals in a month there's an additional office pool of, let's call it $5,000. If you do ten deals, and you're making 50 percent profit, that's $50,000. You just made $50,000, and you weren't even involved. Would you be willing to give $5,000 to get to the fifty? Everybody gets roughly $1,250. That's a big deal to people. They love that recognition.

ROLES

A lead manager's only responsibility is to effectively manage the leads, set the appointments, and get the acquisitions person into the house. The lead manager in a lot of organizations is also responsible for initiating the marketing every month—direct mail, setting up outbound calling campaigns, outbound voicemail campaigns, managing people that are going out and putting up bandit signs, whatever it is. Whatever generates the inbound lead in most cases falls underneath the lead manager.

The acquisitions person has one job: go on as many appointments as they can and get as many contracts in-house as they can. The acquisitions person should be armed with a good outline of how to effectively determine the comparable values of the property ("comps") using all the tools that are available. Our site and Sean Terry's Flip2Freedom Academy are great resources; everything you need is right there.

Dispositions is on the other side of the equation. Their responsibility is to engage the buyers, to maximize the price that you're selling the property for, and make sure that relationship is being nurtured. It is an outbound, outreach job. They are creating anticipation. This person always knows who's ready to buy right now.

The transaction coordinator keeps a transaction moving forward. They work with the title company to make sure the deal is progressing and doesn't fall through.

That's what the team looks like when this thing becomes completely passive to you. And that's it.

CHAPTER 5

WORKING YOURSELF OUT OF A JOB AND INTO A BUSINESS

So far I've explained the reverse wholesaling methodology, how it works from start to finish. I've described setting it up, thinking big picture, and understanding where you want to take your business so that you don't just own a job. That's what successful people do. Most of us are not trained to think that way. We're trained to think in terms of a transaction. We think, "I need to make money. I need to make a deal. I'm highly motivated. My bills are stacking up. I just got laid off. Whatever is in front of my face is what I'm most concerned about." That's just human nature.

You need to keep the endgame in mind if you want to build

a *business*. Understand where you want to go. None of us get into our car and say, "I'm going to the movies tonight, and I'll just drive around until I see a movie theater." It doesn't work like that. We know which movie we want to see, we know where the movie theater is, we know the best route to get there, and we leave early enough so we can get there on time. We have an end in mind.

Building a business is the same thing. If you don't know the destination you're trying to reach, then you are certainly not using the most effective route. I want to give you a very effective, clearly defined route. There's certainly a lot more to it than what I put in these pages, no question; I'm trying to wet your whistle, to make sure you understand that what I'm telling you is entirely possible.

You may be thinking, "All right, I get it. I know I eventually want to build the business. But, right now, I'm just trying to do some deals." Or you may be thinking, "How in the heck do I put somebody in place and trust that they will do deals the way I want them to? Nobody's ever going to care about my business as much as I do." Or maybe you're thinking, "What happens if the people I trust screw up?"

Those are all small-minded thoughts that will ensure that you always own a job rather than owning a business.

To own and operate a business, you need to empower

people to do the job without your involvement. You set it up, and you train them to do the job. You must give them rules. I'll give you ten sample business rules you can use to train somebody over the course of the next thirty, sixty, or ninety days to sit side by side with you. You can give them a piece of every deal that they do. If you train them right, that's literally a deal that you'll get paid on without ever having to be involved. You'll get a piece of somebody else's work and effort. You do that enough times and you won't even have to be involved at all.

The reality is we (my brothers, my father, and I) have very little actual involvement, because we set up a business by empowering our people. We have team members in our office who know exactly how to do the deals the way we would do them. We benefit from not having to be strapped to our work. We're not slaves to our business. We get to work on bigger and better things, like how to grow the business and how to enjoy life. That's what this is about. That's how you become financially free.

Empower people to do their job without your involvement.

Set up "Business Rules" that give them clear boundaries.

Train them to do their job and LET THEM DO IT.

10 SAMPLE BUSINESS RULES

Rule 1: Know Your Minimum Profit. Everybody in your office knows the minimum profit number you're trying to reach. If an opportunity arises, and if it meets the minimum profit number, they have the autonomy and authority to say, "Yes," at this step.

Rule 2: Sell to Cash Buyers. As long as the transaction is being sold to a cash buyer and it meets the minimum profit from above, it is a "Yes." Now, there are exceptions to the rules. You will choose to do deals that are lower than your minimum profit number. You will do deals that are not sold to cash buyers. These are the exceptions and not the rule. These are the only ones that you get personally involved with.

Rule 3: Accept No Contingencies. If a contract comes in with zero contingencies, no inspection clauses, and no other financial contingencies, as long as the other two rules are also met, this is still a "Yes."

Rule 4: Stay Within the Limits: Designate the certain areas that are always good for your team members to say, "Yes," too. The properties should be located within that 60 percent to 80 percent of the city where you operate. Every city has bad areas. As long as your team members are doing deals within that designated area of the cities, they should be empowered to act on that.

Rule 5: Buyers Meet Equity Minimums. Again, you'll certainly do deals where this is not met, but if you can, give your team equity minimums. For example, a deal must have at least 20 percent equity for your buyer left in it. Then that's a good way to empower them to say, "Yes."

Rule 6: Meet Cash Flow Minimums. If you're selling them a property you know that they are going to use as a rental, do the math for them. Help your team understand what the actual cash flow will be and then set minimums for them. For example, it must cash flow at least a hundred dollars a month for our clients for me to say, "Yes."

Rule 7: Meet a Specified Rate of Return. This is similar to the cash flow rule, just a different way of stating it. In that instance, you're looking for a specific cash flow. In this one, you're looking for a specific rate of return. Do the math for them; back into it and help them understand what your minimums would be. For example, we always want our buyers to be able to get a minimum of 8 percent return on their money in a year. If that is the case, then you can say, "Yes," to the deal.

Rule 8: Minimal Rehab. If a property requires $15,000 or less in rehab and a rehab timeline of twenty-one days or less, and all of the other rules above have been met, then this property is a "Yes."

Rule 9: A Sure Closing Term. If all of the rules above have been met and the property can close in thirty days or less, then your team should be good to say, "Yes."

Rule 10: An Easy Buyer Transaction. If you're selling properties that are ultimately going to be rentals, make sure that you're setting up your buyer for an easy transaction. Make sure that there is strong rental demand where they are buying. Make your team understand what's going to happen after this transaction. You're training your team to think like you think, to understand that it's not a transactional business, it is a client business.

Now, if all of those rules are met, then the people in your office should have the autonomy and authority to do a deal without you, because you would do those deals. It's a no-brainer. You can make the rules as loose or as strict as you want. The point is, if you have good rules in place, you're empowering people to do deals without you getting involved. That means that you win: you have a business, not a job.

GET PEOPLE TO WORK FOR NO OUT-OF-POCKET MONEY

Here is a way to get people working for you at no out-of-pocket cost to yourself: you set up all those rules, and then find reliable people, and tell them, "Listen, go follow those steps, and whatever the profit is, I'll give you 25 percent of the first few deals." If you do that, you'll have people working their tail off for you right away to close a deal, and you literally pay them nothing until the sale closes. The only way they get paid is by closing the deal. That's how you get started. That's how you take reverse wholesaling and actually build a business around it.

I want you to be smart. I want you to build a business. I want you to be able to get out of life whatever you want. As long as you own a job, you are nowhere near financially free. What I am sharing with you is all about being efficient and strategic.

People ask us, "How the hell do you do so many deals every month?" It's very simple. We don't buy one thing without clearly understanding when it will be sold. We don't take any risk or any chances on anything. We do enough research on the front end. We build a relationship with the buyers. When we go to market and pull the trigger, we know everything about the target. We do our market research, and we know exactly what our buyers want to buy. We ride those markets and create the deals. We flip the contract very quickly, and we get out of the way.

Once you get that first deal, set aside 50 percent of your profit and invest it right back in your business. Do it again and again to start building momentum. Continue educating yourself. When you start putting people and systems in place that automate the process and you get out of the way, this becomes an amazing passive income stream for you right there.

I have shown you how this requires minimal money, if any. Go out and engage cash buyers as I've shown you, using our system. Then go to every wholesaler, investor, or realtor in the market, and use that leverage and knowledge. Now you can say, "I have a cash buyer that wants to buy." People will bring you every deal they have. That's how you'll get your first deal off the ground. Continue educating yourself. Begin putting people and systems in place that automate the process, and you get out of the way.

I can't make it any simpler than that. I am not telling you that this is easy, but I am telling you this is simple. We have a plan. It works. We are not that smart. You don't have to be that smart, but you have to be willing to go out there and do what's necessary to make it happen.

For some of you this is exactly what you needed to read. Others are looking for something even more passive than this. In the next chapter I explain how to build a rental portfolio anywhere in the country in a completely passive environment.

I'd love to give you additional training information. Go to KentClothier.com/FreeTraining and check out several free videos, as well as an infographic and other training materials that walk you through this entire process, A to Z. There's also a bonus offer to get involved with our software, which will do a lot of this kind of heavy lifting for you very, very easily.

BOOK TWO

How to Purchase Real Estate out of the Area

CHAPTER 6

BLUEPRINT FOR SUCCESS

In this chapter I'm going to describe something that can be passive from the very beginning: investing in Income-Producing Properties all over the country. There are a few steps to making this happen, and there are a few rules that you need to follow. If you follow them, I can assure you that this will be one of the most enriching investments you've ever made, as well as one of the most passive.

Not all real estate markets are created equal. I've broken this chapter into six main tips that you have to implement in order to be successful when purchasing Income-Producing Properties. (I saved the best tip for last, but don't read ahead!)

TIP NUMBER ONE

Get comfortable with the idea of buying and holding property in areas outside of where you live. This will allow you to experience greater cash flow from other markets. Let's face it, the chances of you living in a great cash flow market are pretty slim, so you must understand that you can benefit from other markets remotely.

When you do it correctly, you can safely build a highly profitable real estate portfolio and target very specific markets that will give you the best return—all without living there.

It's amazing that you can experience all these benefits remotely. First, you have to get comfortable with the idea of buying out of area. Buying an investment house is no different than buying a stock. You don't need to visit the company, tour the offices, meet the CEO, or own their products in order to invest in the company. If you're smart, it's a simple investment decision based on data. You gather information, and if it makes sense, you do it.

Warren Buffett doesn't just invest in companies based in Omaha, Nebraska. He knows that not every great deal is in his backyard, so he looks for the best opportunities in the best markets worldwide! When you treat your purchase of Income-Producing Properties the same way, you will put yourself in a position to capitalize on better markets. Here's a great example. I live in San Diego, California, where a

2,000 square foot house could go for as much as several million dollars because of how close the houses are to the ocean.

That same house, built with the same materials, the same age, in the exact same condition, in a great neighborhood in Dallas, Texas might sell for $100,000.

That means that Dallas property has a chance of cash flowing. If the only place I invested in was San Diego, I'd be hard pressed to find a single Income-Producing Property. That's why I live in one place and invest in others. This is how you start building real wealth in a passive way, instead of working your fingers to the bone to create a little extra income and only looking in your own backyard for "deals."

Now with that said, do not just run out and purchase property in *any city* without doing some research FIRST. (Avoid this BIG MISTAKE.) I used to believe that it was all about the property! If it was cheap and the rents were good, then I could make money. Now I know better, and so do you. A property is only good if it meets several other criteria.

Here's what will happen if you buy any property in any city and make the mistake I am about to describe. You'll begin to lose money! Many "smart investors" have run into bad cities and bought up questionable properties, only to find out that they were now "hung out to dry." Go read up on some of the hedge funds that ran into places like Detroit and Cleveland, bought up everything in sight and are now regretting that decision.

TIP NUMBER TWO

Here's what you do instead: **Do research on cities that are growing.** Find cities where there were no major swings in appreciation or depreciation in real estate prices, where the job market is steady, and the economic outlook is positive. If a city is growing and has good middle-income job creation, then it's worth considering. We spend a great deal of time understanding the markets that we operate in. Memphis, Dallas, St. Louis, Little Rock, Oklahoma City, and Houston are all great markets for our clients and us because they have a strong job market, economic stability, and a steady rental market. We've done all of the research and we know that none of these markets experienced dramatic swings when the real estate market collapsed. They were slow and steady the whole way.

For example, we know that FedEx is the major employer in Memphis. We know that over 50 percent of the population rents and we know that the median house price is roughly $100,000. We know what is driving the economy, where the growth is headed, and where we need to be focused on finding ideal properties for our tenant base. We know the homes that our prospective tenants would like to rent.

We also know the homes that our investor clients would be proud to own. These things matter and, in the end, will make for a much better investment in rental properties.

Doing some basic research will allow you to feel more comfortable with the idea that these markets represent a sound investment vehicle. Focus on investing in smart real estate markets that give you the best monthly return on investment and the ability to minimize your risk. The benefits of this simple tip continue to astound me and the thousands I've given it to. That brings me to our next tip, which goes hand in hand with the first two. When you get comfortable with the fact that there are better cash flow markets out there and you do some research to find them, then the next tip makes perfect sense.

TIP NUMBER THREE

Avoid the "Rental Nightmares" by focusing on providing rental properties for your "Average American Family." Unfortunately, most of us associate "renters" with the horror stories that we've either lived or heard about; stories of people's property being torn up, renters being late with payments, clogged up toilets, late-night maintenance calls, etc.

I get it. We've all heard those stories. That's not what I'm talking about here. None of us want to be slumlords or own any property that we wouldn't be proud to call our own.

On the contrary, what I'm talking about is focusing on the huge market that has been recently created and largely ignored. Millions of great people were caught up in the recession and financial meltdown that our country suffered through. For one reason or another, they were forced to leave their homes and officially pushed into the national renter pool. These are people who in some cases never have rented before. They've always owned their home. They've always taken care of it, treated it well, and taken pride in ownership. Now they are looking for a nice home to rent, raise their family, and treat the home the same way.

This is where you come in. Providing great homes, at great rents, to these great tenants is a win-win-win situation. It's also a gold mine for you as you build your portfolio of Income- Producing Properties. When you understand the market, you're focused on the right city, with the right economic factors driving growth and good jobs to the right people. Focus on providing those people with the right property. That's when the magic happens—rental properties in the right city to the right people. People who pay their rents on time, take care of your property, and provide a generally better experience for you as a landlord.

Can things still go wrong? Of course they can. I'd be insane to claim that you will never have a problem. What I am saying is that this approach is logical, it's methodical, it's proven, and it is more likely to put you in a better position all around. After we learned the importance of these first three tips, my family and I began applying this to our own portfolios. At the time of this book's publication, our properties produce over $104,000 in monthly income. Again: Rental properties first, then market, then client. Those are the first three tips for our Blueprint for Success.

TIP NUMBER FOUR

Learn to evaluate and "comp" properties correctly. This ties in directly with the previous three tips. If you are investing in Income-Producing Properties in a market that you have researched, and for the right client base, then you have to evaluate the value of these properties differently. You have to evaluate your investments based on the income that they produce for you—period. *Nothing else.*

Many new investors get caught in the trap of evaluating their real estate investments based on the same methodology that they would determine the value of their own home. They look online and do some research on Zillow, Realtor.com, or any of the other online websites that estimate property values. They come up with a value based on what one of these sites says it's "worth."

In order to understand this mistake, you have to know how these sites make their money. They are designed for advertisers—not for the accuracy of their data.

These sites generate revenue by advertisers spending money on their sites. Their sole purpose as a company is to get people to look at their site for as long as they can. Their purpose is not to create accurate data for our industry. These sites are not held to industry standards by any measure. If they were, then why in the world would banks, lenders, and borrowers spend *billions* each year on appraisals if all they had to do was look online and get the information for free? Plus, these sites are constantly looking backwards (what the neighbor's house sold for), instead of looking ahead at what the property will produce in cash flow. Not to mention that in some cases the values are based on properties prior to them being repaired, rehabbed, and generally fixed up.

If we know the values are wrong and we know that serious investors don't use these sites, then you do not need to either.

Smart investors do not only look backwards to establish the value of a property. Instead, they value a property based on its income potential. If smart investors do it this way, then so should you.

Here's what I mean. If a property is completely rehabilitated (fixed up to current standards and beautiful) and is currently rented at or above market rents, then that property is *absolutely* more valuable than what Zillow or other sites would propose. Why? Because again, these sites are only looking at historical sales data on every home in the neighborhood, including the properties sold at a discount. These sites have no way of quantifying that your investment property has been fixed up, is now the most beautiful home in the neighborhood, *and* is producing monthly income. So, keep it simple and focus on the math.

A good rule of thumb that I personally use is the 1 percent rule. Take the monthly rental income and multiply it by one hundred. If it's a great property, with a long-term lease, in a great neighborhood, then a month's rent realistically represents about 1 percent of the property's value (that's why you multiply by one hundred). Example: If the monthly rent is $1,200 a month and all the conditions that I laid out previously are true, then the property is probably worth somewhere in the neighborhood of $120,000. Even if Zillow or some other bone-headed site says it's worth $95,000, it's worth $120,000 because it's creating a 12 percent gross cash on cash annual return. End of story.

This is that smart guy thinking, versus dumb guy thinking: looking for the cheapest house in any city, with no tenant profile, and no plan. If you make enough of these smart investing decisions over time, you'll quietly build a real estate portfolio that will pay big dividends over many, many years.

Imagine what your life will feel like when you master

this: monthly checks rolling in while you own an Income-Producing Property that is a hard asset for building long-term wealth. Just imagine being able to create a passive income of $5,000, $10,000, or even $15,000 a month by investing in smart, Income-Producing Properties. Imagine that it doesn't stop. These are assets. They can and should outlive you. You can pass this Income-Producing portfolio on to your kids and grandkids—for generations to come. These are Income-Producing Properties that, depending on how you purchase them, you may immediately own free and clear, or with debt that will be paid down over the next few years from the rental income, and then you'll soon own them.

Free and clear.

See the shock and surprise in the eyes of your friends, family, and colleagues as you go from struggling to put enough money away each month to being a real estate mogul with a portfolio of properties around the country producing income, building wealth, and all professionally managed, maintained, and profitable.

TIP NUMBER FIVE

Educate yourself on the power of leverage, creative financing options, and advantageous tax strategies. This was a real eye-opener for me and my entire family.

For years we used traditional financing to purchase properties. In some cases we just used our own cash. We quickly came to appreciate the power of creative financing and some of the investing strategies of the superrich. There are literally hundreds of ways to finance the purchase of Income-Producing Properties, and you need to know as many of them as possible. Learning to invest with your Self-Directed IRA, Solo 401(k), or other retirement accounts can create tax-free or tax-deferred benefits that can play a huge role in your portfolio growth year over year.

In addition, accessing third-party funding for your deals only compounds your return on investment and allows you to purchase more Income-Producing Properties, creating even more monthly income. These techniques are critical to your future growth.

Check this out.

Over the last five years, I've watched a member of my own family purchase twenty-five properties and put them all on fifteen-year notes. He takes none of the cash flow each month. Instead, he pays the notes down, reducing the principal owed each month.

His plan is to own them all free and clear in fifteen years, when he is forty years old.

He'll have an income of $25,000 a month with no debt on the properties at all because it's all been paid off over the last fifteen years—*when he's forty.*

He'll pay some property taxes, some insurance, and a little maintenance, all from the $25,000 a month he is taking in. That was five years ago. He's now five years closer to that exact scenario: forty years old with passive income of $300,000 a year.

That's the power of tips one thru five. Now, I told you that I'd save the best for last, and I have. Tip number six is absolutely the most important piece of this entire puzzle. This is the one thing that makes it all work.

TIP NUMBER SIX

Find the right partners. This is actually a very simple argument to make. Smart investors know that without smart people around them they are dead in the water. It requires a team to make your investments pay dividends time and time again. Even if you go into the right market, do all of your research, find the right tenant bases, and find the properties, you still have to finance, purchase, and rehab the property, then screen the tenants, show the property, and get it rented. All before you can make a single dollar on your investment. This shows the importance of your partners. You need partners who understand your needs, your desired outcomes, your investment strategy, and how to help you to make it a reality.

Here are some of the partners that you will need in the markets where you invest:

- Wholesaler
- Realtor
- Closing Attorney
- Rehabber
- Property Manager
- Insurance Agent
- Project Manager
- Local Bank and/or Lenders
- Title Company

Your wholesalers and realtors can find you the properties. You will pay them a commission or markup on every deal that you purchase. Now, it's safe to assume that the best deals are all going to need a little bit of work, so your project manager and rehab crew should submit bids for all of the rehab costs in writing. You should be able to clearly see the markup that they are charging you for their services. Your property management company will charge you 10 percent or so to pick up the rent checks and send money to you. The right local partner or partners will make all of the difference in the world!

These partners make this whole thing tick for you. Without them, it's not even worth getting started.

I guarantee these six tips will save you a ton of time, and help to make you more money, *if you apply them*. When you take these six tips, you can develop your very own Blueprint for Success.

CHAPTER 7

HOW TO CHOOSE A GREAT INVESTMENT MARKET

Do you remember tip number one in the previous chapter? "Be comfortable investing in properties outside of where you live." Let's get started.

Cheap houses don't make a great market. In fact, we often tell investors, "Forget the house." Don't even look at the house yet. Make sure you know the market first. The condition of the market you are investigating will dictate whether you decide to invest or not. What good is a "cheap house" if the market is no good?

When investigating a market, dig into the details of the area. This is a place where investors can get bogged down in details that can leave them unable to make a decision because the research never ends. It's analysis paralysis.

Analysis Paralysis

I'm not advocating that! This research should amount to one evening on a computer, at most. It is not that difficult to research an area. You will always be able to check out your conclusions in person, but before you go off flying all over the country, do a little research.

Start with a long-term outlook in a market. Take a look at population. Is it going up? Is it going down? The importance of investing in a growing area cannot be overstated. Make sure you look at the MSA (Metro Statistical Area) as well, and not just the city. America is so spread out through urban sprawl today that you want to know what is going on with all the surrounding bedroom communities, too.

Your city may be small or may be big, but we like areas that are growing. I want to own investment properties as a generational wealth-building tool because eventually these properties are for my children. I want them to be located in a vibrant area that's growing.

Look at key industries in an area as well, from an economic standpoint. What's happening with jobs? Not the unemployment rate, but are there net positive jobs being created in a market each year? Every city will have ups and downs, and every city loses companies to closure, moving, and downsizing. That is a fact of the current business climate. What we want to know is, are there businesses moving in? Are major companies, major employers, different areas of development, and different industries showing interest in a city?

Those are key questions that tell me, as an investor, whether the city has good long-term viability. We want to know not only what is happening today, but what can we expect from the future. You cannot get that information from an unemployment rate. You have to get into it and read about it.

Search out and read up on local city bloggers. You will find all types, from business bloggers, to recreational enthusiasts, to local moms who like to share about their city. There are a ton of blogs out there for every city and they are a great place to get an inside feel. Skim a few. Do not spend time loading up on every detail that a blogger writes about. Instead, get a feel for what is happening. The chamber of commerce is always going to give you the rosiest picture and best news. That's an okay place to start, but make sure you balance it out with a real-world feel from the blogs. This will help you determine if it's a place to invest your money for the long term. Always remember that your task is getting a feel for the city. If you feel no connection at all and do not see the long-term opportunity, strike it from your list. If you love it or even have good feelings, but are not sure, that is a city that deserves more research.

Dig into some of the finer details, like what's going on with housing prices overall. Not just the investment prices, but overall. Are houses moving quickly through the MLS? How long are they sitting on the market? Are sellers being forced to take a discount from the list price on final contract price?

These simple questions allow you to look inside a market and get an idea of what is happening with housing. How about housing starts? Are they up or are they down? You might even type a Google query of "how many sales are to investors in XYZ."

Investigate the pricing history for that market by looking at certain factors, such as what the highest price in that market was compared to what prices are today. You're looking for a large variance. You're looking for a very high peak, compared to a low price today.

What percentage of sales are foreclosures? The presence of foreclosures does not necessarily mean it will be a good long-term investing market. It is simply an indication of available properties where an investor may be able to buy at a discount.

Finally, what does it cost to live in that market? We're always looking for a market that has a relatively low cost of living. Specifically, we look for markets where the average cost of housing is not more than three times the average income of someone who lives there. That will be a market where the house is still affordable. As an investor, you can still buy a house, rent it, and make a return, even if you have to use a property management company.

As you can see, a lot of numbers go into making a great market and none of those numbers are about cheap houses. Unfortunately, cheap is a state of mind that has hurt more real estate investors than any other single factor.

The house is always the last thing we look at, and never before we know the long-term viability of a market. Too many investors are buying investment properties in out-of-area markets because the property is cheap. When we get calls from investors asking for help with these cheap houses, we ask them, "Cheap compared to what?" Cheap compared to where you live does not mean it's a good deal. Cheap for the city you are buying in does not mean it is a good deal. There are so many more questions you have to answer before you can buy a property. That is why I tell investors to forget about the house!

Forget the House

- ☑ Population/MSA
- ☑ Net positive jobs
- ☑ City bloggers
- ☑ MLS
  - ◆ Prices
  - ◆ Quick sales?
- ☑ Housing starts
- ☑ Pricing history
- ☑ Foreclosures %
- ☑ Cost of living

CHAPTER 8

CHOOSING THE RIGHT TEAM

The right team, especially when you are investing out of area, is extremely important. We invest a lot in our own market, as well as a couple of other markets around the country, but no matter where we're investing we don't do it on our own. We're always looking for someone else to handle the essential services. This is a critical part of my business plan, as I want to leverage the time and talent of others around me to build my passive income. Even when I invest in my own city, I leverage the time and talents of our team.

As investors, we have other things to do in our daily life. When we're investing in real estate, we want to hire the best to handle everything for us. Usually this is a team. You will find it is much easier to manage one person (the team leader) than to manage each individual person. Oftentimes, those teams are called turnkey vendors.

Here are the questions to ask as you seek the right turn-key vendor.

DO THEY UNDERSTAND INVESTORS?

What we mean by that is, are they investors themselves? It takes someone who has been in the trenches and gone through the ins and outs, the good and the bad of being a real estate investor, to fully understand and know what other investors want. This is a *major* sticking point!

What makes an especially good team is if their leader has invested out of area before. Why? They often have experiences that help them improve upon their service, so that you yourself get a better quality. They need to know what is going on in the mind of an investor. What an investor cares about. What an investor worries about at night. What makes investors feel more comfortable? Whose houses are they selling?

Make sure you protect yourself when you're buying houses from out of area by determining that the sellers sell their own properties. Too often, individuals and companies simply sell other people's properties either by tying them up with a contract or selling properties for a commission. You don't want to buy from someone who is selling someone else's properties for a commission. The most obvious reason to avoid this is that they are not in control of the property, and more to the point, they cannot tell you the details of the property. You certainly don't want to buy from a company that is simply selling properties off the MLS. That leaves you open to wasting time, spinning your wheels, and losing properties.

DO THEY HAVE BUSINESS PROCESSES SET UP TO MAKE LIFE EASIER FOR YOU?

This is what we call the business-oriented real estate company. Usually the background of the owners may be in another industry or in some other related field, but not necessarily the real estate industry. Some of the most successful companies out there are owned by entrepreneurs and set up by people who understand business much more than they understand real estate.

Do they:

- Purchase properties?
- Renovate properties?
- Market properties?
- Manage properties?

You are looking for a business where the owners have experience setting up systems and training people. Real estate happens to be the product they build their company around, but they know how to set up a great business. The business should be predicated and built on great service, great organization, great structure, so that you have a successful investing experience. That's what we have looked for and built. We want to work with a group that conducts itself like a well-run company. We like to see organization and a flow where every employee serves a purpose and has a function that helps us succeed.

We have spoken with and come across a number of companies through the years where the mentality is "stay small and keep it all!" There is nothing wrong with that attitude, but it makes it very difficult for me as a long distance investor to believe that there is enough staff to handle the situations that will always come up. Some see this as personal preference. We simply see it as common sense. If I am going to purchase a property out of area, especially across the country, I want to know the company I am buying from has a business-minded owner looking out for me.

DO THEY OWN AND OPERATE ALL ASPECTS OF THE BUSINESS?

When I talk about being a business-oriented company, I mean a company that is set up for your success. Investors have the most success when they work with companies that own and operate every piece of the equation. They don't outsource, they don't choose third-party companies to provide a service for them. They handle everything in-house for the investor.

This is a key service for an out-of-area investor because it gives you one contact for everything that goes on in the process of purchasing an investment property, not three, four, or five different contacts per house. That piece of this equation will help you make money, because you won't spend time spinning your wheels. Making one call is always better than having to make a whole list of calls.

WHAT'S BEEN THEIR BIGGEST REAL ESTATE INVESTING MISTAKE?

Ask that question looking for a little honesty, a little openness. Good businesses are the ones who can tell you when they have failed and how that failure shaped their success today. They should be in tune with the things they have done in the past that they don't want to repeat, and more importantly they should be in tune with the mistakes they don't want you to repeat as an investor.

If people tell you that they've never made a mistake in investing, it is up to you if you want to believe them. If someone can lay their past out for you, saying, "Here are the mistakes I've made," you know what else they will be able to tell you? "Here's the remedy I put in place to prevent making that mistake again. Here's how I prevent investors from making the same mistakes that I've made."

That's a great way to judge the character and the integrity of someone with whom you want to do business. It's an important question that leads to other questions. It leads to conversations and a chance to build a relationship based on trust. Plenty of good owners will tell you about their mistakes as personal investors and as a company. If you want to choose the right company, then you have to be able to ask the hard questions and listen to the answers they give you.

CHAPTER 9

CHOOSING THE RIGHT HOUSE

Price is what you pay. Value is what you get!

You have the right *market*, and you feel like you have the right *team*. It's now down to the *houses*.

Charlie Munger, Warren Buffett's right-hand man, said something really valuable. I'm paraphrasing here, but it went like this: "So often, investors tell me about these really, really cheap houses they can find, whether it's in my market or their market, or anywhere around the country. I ask them, 'How do you define cheap?'"

Cheap is one of those words that truly scare us. Is it cheap because it's a low price for the market you're buying in, or is it cheap because you could never find that house in your market? It really doesn't matter. Select houses that are the right price for where you are buying. Does the price come with the appropriate amount of risk for you? Just because it's *cheap* doesn't mean it's *good*.

Always look for value. Value is defined in a lot of different ways by investors, but for me value means that we are buying the right house, for the right price, in the right market, with the right team that will get me the right return. I'm always looking to find houses that make sense and that fit nicely inside my portfolio.

Whether I'm buying my first house or my twenty-first house, I want to make sure my long-term goals are met. Ask yourself the big question: "Are the reasons for buying this house aligned with the value I get from it?"

The best way to answer that question is to break it down.

CHAPTER 10

PAPER RETURNS VS. REAL-LIFE RETURNS

I had an investor tell me that he gets over 20 percent return on everything he buys, but that's after he includes the appreciation he gets each year. Of course, he has no idea if his property is appreciating, but he likes to add a conservative number (whatever that is) to his calculations.

Whether that investor is right or wrong, this is an example of how you can manipulate numbers to make your returns look fantastic. Companies, too, can do a lot of different things on paper to determine what kind of return you will get as an investor. What's on paper looks great, but the reality is more valuable than the perception, when it comes to making any informed decisions.

When we review our expected returns on an investment property, we look at our hard costs. We want to know exactly what taxes, insurance, and principal and interest (if we're using leverage) are going to be on that property. We call these hard costs because you know they are coming each and every month. Once we know these costs, we know exactly how to factor our return.

We are big believers in talking one-on-one with a company and finding out how they keep soft costs (maintenance and vacancies) down. Don't just plug in some figure and tell me, "This is what we think it could be." We want to know what the averages are for an entire portfolio.

We want to know what other investors are experiencing with move-outs and monthly repairs. What is the turnkey company doing to improve my bottom line? I'm looking for properties or processes that can lower the soft costs as much as possible. How does the company plan to keep those costs low? That could include high-level renovations that eliminate deferred maintenance, or tenant services, or both. Without the ability to hold down costs, any possibility of hitting sky-high paper returns is impossible. Make sure you include soft costs, are always thinking about them, and that the company you are dealing with has answers in place for holding them down.

Guarantees Are a Red Flag

One of the big no-nos, and the biggest red flags, is guarantees. Not every guarantee is done with a sinister intent, but in our experience, most guarantees are in place not for the benefit of the investor, but for the benefit of the company selling the property.

The guarantees we're talking about are, "Guaranteed twelve months of rent in the first year," or, "Guaranteed no-maintenance costs in the first year." It doesn't matter how long the amount of time is. The question to ask is, if that guarantee were not in place, how would that property perform?

If the guaranteed rent were not in place, would the property go vacant in the first year? If the no-maintenance guarantee were not in place, would there be maintenance during that first year? There is a big difference between a guarantee that represents being willing to stand behind your work, and a guarantee that inflates first year returns and hides what's going to happen after year one.

Don't allow a guarantee to sway you into buying a property or change the numbers in your mind. Always calculate what will take place if that guarantee was not there.

CHAPTER 11

ALWAYS BUY NEIGHBORHOOD NORMAL

You have probably been told that you should never buy a two-bedroom, one-bath house. When an investor tells me this, I'll present to them a scenario where I think it makes sense.

Let's say the house is near a university. The price point versus the rent you can get makes sense. You want to add it to your portfolio, but you've been told, "Never buy two-bedroom, one-bath homes." You look around the neighborhood and every home in the area, because it's near a university, is a two-bedroom, one-bath. In that scenario, would you buy it? Most investors say yes, because it's normal to that neighborhood.

You should never buy a two-bedroom, one-bath home in a neighborhood of three-bedroom, two-bath, two-car garage homes. That's the value of that aphorism. A more valuable rule of thumb is, always buy what makes sense for that neighborhood.

Buy Neighborhood Normal

We only buy properties that make sense in their neighborhood, that match the other properties. If every other home around a neighborhood has a two-car garage, we should buy with a two-car garage, too. Otherwise we would be outside the neighborhood normal.

If you want more information on how to get started immediately, someone from our team will do a free, one-hour consultation about what you hope to accomplish by building a passive rental portfolio, and even supplying the properties and all the services to you. Go to TheInvestorConcierge.com/VIP, fill out all the questions, then we will call you in the next forty-eight hours. No commitment, just support!

BOOK THREE

How to Be a Private Lender

CHAPTER 12

WHY PRIVATE LENDING?

I've explained two sources of passive income: reverse wholesaling and cash flow on properties outside of your area. Let's get to the most passive, bad-ass way of investing in real estate, a way that delivers fantastic returns on your investment without lifting a hammer.

My family started private lending around 2012. We had "dead money" sitting in self-directed IRAs earning pretty much nothing or, in some instances, losing money. Our plan was to do something with that money, but we got busy and it sat there, waiting to be revived.

We decided that saving it is not the answer—growing it was the answer. We started working with people who we had trained over the years, and were comfortable with, and knew what their business was about. We understood what they were doing in real estate.

They needed money to help fund their growth, so we started lending to them in Alabama, Texas, Florida, California, Tennessee, and Arizona. We financed their deals on a regular basis, and that continues today.

When you're a private lender, it's very important that you understand the rules of the game because there are a lot of ways you can get hurt. Private lending only works if you are crossing your t's and dotting your i's, surrounding yourself with good people, and making sure you're doing your due diligence. When you do those things, it is an amazing return on investment. If you don't do those things, it'll be nothing but a nightmare.

In order to answer the question of "why private lending?" we first have to look at the traditional source of funds for real estate investing: banks. Their purpose is not to make money *for* us, but *from* us. Banks serve as middlemen who control other people's money. Currently, they typically pay us less than 1 percent on our deposits, then turn around and loan it out at a 4 percent to 6 percent rate or higher. Many people believe it's safe to keep your money in a bank, and they're right. It's secure, it's easy, and the risk is limited. But it's also a dismal way to make money. Banks follow established rules created by the banking structure. It is legal for them to pay out a lower rate of interest, while they make a higher rate of return. Well, guess what? It's also legal for us (and you) to do the same thing. In other words, we can be a bank and lend money out based on opportunities we choose, with connections we make.

WHAT IS PRIVATE LENDING?

In this case, you're acting as a private bank, loaning your own money against a secured asset—real estate. You're loaning your own funds to others who meet your criteria for a good lending investment. You can also jointly use your funds with other people, friends or associates, to make loans as you choose. (You are limited to lending to businesses, not consumers. That's a different scenario. We never lend directly to consumers because there are very complex laws that make that difficult to do.)

Private lending provides an alternative investment space, very different from traditional investments like stocks, bonds, mutual funds, annuities. You have greater control over your investments. How much control do you really have when you're investing in a stock or a bond? How much control over the management or decision making do you have there? None, nada, nothing. You just have to hope the company is doing well.

There are a lot of investment opportunities in this entrepreneurial world of private investing in real estate. What we're doing is filling a void left by the conventional market that can't keep pace. The banking institutions, where most people get loans to run business or to buy real estate, are very much a controlled environment. The government has many regulations. Banks cannot just wheel and deal at their whim. There's a void. There's a place, a middle sector, where it takes entrepreneurs to come in and solve real problems for people who can take properties and bring them back to the market, rehab them, and create a habitable place. We provide that capital. It's a great opportunity if you want to control your own investments.

There's relatively little competition in this private lending sector. Very few people understand it. When most people think about investing in real estate, they think about shows like *Flip This House*. They think about owning a property, fixing it up, and having contractors and tenants. Certainly, that can be done, but private lending has specific advantages that those who invest in real property don't have. The other cool thing about it is, as an individual, you face no special licensing or certification requirements so long as you're lending to businesses and not consumers.

Great returns are possible, much greater than what you can get with banks today. You can invest as a lender and see returns of 8 percent, 9 percent, 10 percent, 11 percent, and 12 percent, safe and secure, as opposed to having money in the bank at their measly 1 percent or 1.5 percent. Your investment accounts continue to grow. These great returns allow you to achieve proper returns based on your risk tolerance and the opportunity that you can make available to you by following the lessons in this section of the book.

Private lending is also a launching point: it's a great way to learn more about real estate. If you always wanted to get involved in real estate, but you don't feel like you have the time and expertise to deal with the property, contractors, and tenants, learning how to lend your money through other people's deals is a great way to learn the documentation. Lending also gives you an opportunity to have equity positions, or equity ownership, which I'll talk about a bit later.

You have direct control over your money. You have sole discretion over the deals you decide to do or decline. The property and the people you want to work with are totally up to you. You get to make your own decisions. You get to set the rate of return that you feel is appropriate for the money you're going to invest, the potential risk you're thinking about taking, and the opportunity in the marketplace. You get to decide that. *He who has the gold makes the rules.*

The terms of the deal, how long you leave your money in place and when the payments come in, are all defined and established by you. You control the duration of the loan. You decide all the criteria.

Banks	Stocks Bonds	Private Lender
Pays low interest charges high interest	No control over performance	Secured by collateral

As a private lender, you hold what's called a lien position. It's a secured position found in the public records against the property. That lien position gives you certain rights, but no obligation to maintain the property, fix the property, or deal with plumbing or tenants. Think about it. Banks and private lenders do not get called to fix issues with the property. You can make money by owning the loan—or paper, as it's called in the industry. You deal with property managers. In other words, you don't have to own the property to make money on it. You hold a legal right without the ongoing expenses or headaches. You're able to get your capital invested and you don't have to deal with all the moving parts of owning real estate. It's a great place to be.

Real estate assets secure your funds. Your money is backed by collateral, a specific property or properties. If the borrower, for any reason, defaults on their payments, you have the right and the ability to collect on that loan by taking back that specific property. Real estate is what we call a tangible asset. Wall Street stocks, bonds, mutual funds—those are paper assets. Those can be okay investments, but there's no security there. If a company goes broke, or if a company doesn't pay on their debt or their bond, you have very little recourse at all. With real estate, you have specific collateral.

You have to go into this business with eyes wide open, realizing that statistically speaking, if you loan enough money over the years, at some point you're probably going to run into trouble and have to take a property back. It's just bound to happen, and that's a little bit frustrating.

The good news is, private lending allows for a strong control factor. We can set our terms, our criteria, and the duration of the investment. If we don't like the way a borrower is performing, we can take control. We can actually remove that borrower. You can't do that when you own stocks or bonds. The stock market is regulated by the financial industry and is subject to multiyear cycles. We can't control those cycles. With private lending, I'll show you how you can hedge against those cycles so you don't have the volatility involved in your investments.

With private lending, you can adjust your returns to fit the market and your risk tolerance. That means that every market has different opportunities. Sometimes there's more money available and less deal flow. Sometimes there's more deal flow and less money. You get to adjust and be aware of what the market conditions provide and fit to suit what you desire for return on your money, your time, and your capital. This also allows you to control and maintain financial safety over your investment capital.

CHAPTER 13

THE INEFFICIENT TRUTH

Private lending is what's called an inefficient market. The stock market, by contrast, is what we call an efficient market. Why? Information in the stock market is available at light speed. People can trade in seconds. There's no lack of distribution of the opportunities, so everything happens all at once.

In real estate, it's completely different. Real estate is very localized. There's not the efficiency of real time information; people have to dig in, talk to other people, and do their due diligence. It's not a scalable investing platform. That's where the opportunity comes in. The information you need to make real estate investment decisions doesn't come from one source of data. Little to no data are instantly available. Answers require manual searches and questioning.

The real opportunities come to us in the real estate sector

through the people we know. That's where the good deals come from. That's where we find out who has a good opportunity. There's no central database. Your ability to put together a team and build a network is critical, but then you have an opportunity that you can't miss.

Growing a network is inefficient but worth your time if you want the benefit of growing your money faster than in any other secured investment. As you know, growing organically, through association with other people and where you hang out, is critical for success. Many of the connections and relationships you make will come from engaging in conversations with people who are the "boots on the ground," the people who deal strictly with the property: contractors, investors, landlords, management companies, and title companies. All these people deal on a regular basis with people who are in the flow of the deal. Knowing these people and letting them know what you do—you have money to lend—creates opportunity. Those are the conversations you want to have on a regular basis.

Big business and banks ignore private lending because it's not scalable. It's local. It requires the inefficiencies of creating conversations in a network. Regulations make it very difficult for big banks to get involved in what we can do on a small basis.

There's a great dependency in business on technology and

instant data access to make a scalable platform. Since that's not present here, there's a great opportunity for you as the individual. The absence of big banks leaves a vast area of opportunity. It's the gap in the marketplace, where we can get our capital involved in earning great returns. It's an entire marketplace that's underserved, and under the radar.

Generally, when we think about the retail real estate arena, we think about brokers and agents, and people who deal with homeowners on a retail basis. Those people are well served, in most cases by the traditional banking sector. Private lending is not about those well-served people; it's about the problem solvers, the people who deal with properties that need to be rehabbed, or have been taken back by banks, or are in bad condition. Sellers are motivated to sell them. You can lend your money to people who are putting these properties back in the marketplace—something the big banks are slow to do.

Big deals and profits are attainable and abundant on a smaller basis for the individual. They are there for us to take advantage of. There's a plethora of smaller deals overlooked by the banks and the bigger institutional money. Individuals, not companies, better manage this gap in the marketplace.

Since the last downturn in 2008, we saw a lot of money coming in the marketplace, printed by the Federal Reserve.

This money was looking for a home. Some of it went to the stock market. A lot of it went to the real estate markets.

Hedge funds decided, "Well, let's go into real estate." We saw them trying to enter the space by buying a lot of foreclosed inventory. They quickly found out that the boots-on-the-ground type of work was very difficult. Many of those hedge funds have since pulled back out of the market because it doesn't work without the right infrastructure. You can't just throw money at it and hope it sticks. You need people to make it happen. They found out that success requires the small entrepreneur who is involved in taking care of the problems. There will always be problems, whether we're in an up cycle, or we're in a down cycle. There's always opportunity. Every cycle has them. You, as the private lender, have the flexibility to loan out small or large amounts of money. You can use small amounts in a retirement account. You can use tax-paid money. You could combine forces with other people and jointly lend money.

Your only limitation is your own personal resources, your network, and your risk level, which you will learn about in a few pages. You'll be able to mitigate risk and learn where your comfort level is. Literally, you can loan out anything from a few thousand dollars to millions of dollars through private lending. It just becomes a matter of your opportunity and what you do with your network.

This inefficiency in the marketplace creates a real need. Entrepreneurs and businesses have real estate inventory that needs immediate financial infusions. Again, taking care of property that needs to be rehabbed or put back on the market is not something that the big banks do very well. They're slow. They're clumsy. They have committees. They have underwriting. They need financial statements. They need appraisals. They need lots of time to make a loan decision.

This doesn't work in the entrepreneurial world. That's where we come in as private lenders, with our associations, our networks, and our understanding of due diligence. The next chapters will teach you how you can be a part of this great opportunity that allows us to help the entrepreneurs, the rehabbers, and the joint venture partners deal with vacant homes, foreclosures, distressed owners who have property that they can't sell because it needs to be rehabbed and can't be listed on the Multiple Listing Service.

Rehabbers, who are constantly taking properties that need to be fixed up and put back on the market, need our help with capital infusions. There are also sellers who need to sell quickly—perhaps they need to move, or for health reasons, or divorce. Many issues create opportunities in which the banks cannot get involved. Entrepreneurs, who are busy rehabbing houses, cannot wait three to six months for a loan committee to make funds available for an acquisition of a property that needs to be rehabbed. They need to be able to do it quickly. That's where the deals are made.

As I like to say, "Money loves speed." Entrepreneurs rely on expediency. In a marketplace where entrepreneurs are solving problems in the real estate sector, there's a need to move quickly. There are properties that we want to be involved in. We want to lend our money on these properties because they're good deals.

Banks can't move rapidly, because of their size, the regulations, the stipulations for underwriting, committees, and financial underwriting. They also have loan limits. You have the opportunity to navigate this inefficiency in the marketplace. Banks can't do it. They miss the whole opportunity. You could step in quickly with your capital, your network, your associations, and service this ignored industry. Your service directly aids the economic engine. Small business entrepreneurs are those who actually create the engine for our country. It's not the big institutions. It's not the big corporations. People with problems always want a quick solution and they will pay a premium, or in many cases, they will discount the sale of an asset to solve that problem. Creating your network will enable you to access these opportunities. Your network is the key to your success in private lending.

CHAPTER 14

YOUR KEY TEAM MEMBERS

A team is so important in everything we do in life, and private lending is no different. Just as I mentioned in the first section of this book, you cannot do it all yourself—and you don't want to because then you're in a job, not owning a business. If you try to do everything yourself, manage all the little moving parts that we'll talk about, then you'll drive yourself crazy. Your team will be a critical piece of your success. To help get you there, I want you to understand the insurance rules and responsibilities, and develop a plan for finding and qualifying your team members.

If you don't have the right people around you to service the loan, the entire process can get exasperating. Ninety-nine percent of the time, things are going to be great. It's that 1 percent that is challenging. You have to be realistic and understand that small errors may come up, but with the right team, issues can be addressed quickly and effectively.

Let's get started with your team.

CERTIFIED PUBLIC ACCOUNTANT, CPA

This person is very helpful because there will always be tax ramifications to any kind of investment, and private lending is no different. The CPA will help you determine your business structure so that you can mitigate and keep the greatest amount of your profit and pay the lowest taxes. They will also help you position your money with proper entities, maybe an LLC, a partnership, a corporation, or a trust.

If you're just getting started, don't get too wound up trying to go after huge deals. It's okay to do a few deals without jumping overboard. What I'm saying here is that, sometimes, people spend a lot of time just getting ready to get ready to do something; at some point, you have to take some action. Remember the analysis paralysis concept I spoke about earlier? If you have an opportunity, go ahead and make your first small deal. Come back after the fact, take your deal to your CPA and say, "Okay, now what should I do with the next deal?" That would be a good way for you to start.

THE ATTORNEY

Private lending involves a lot of legal documents, so this is an important person to have lined up on the front end. Don't let that scare you. You don't have to be the expert here. You'll learn as you go. If you have a good attorney who understands real estate documents, they will keep you safe. They will make sure everything is documented the way it should be for a typical real estate closing (in this case, you're the lender). There are specific documents, and the attorney will walk you through and check all the boxes, so you don't have to worry. You can sleep at night, and your money will be safe.

There are two primary documents that ensure you are repaid and your money is secured against collateral. Those two instruments are (1) the promissory note, and (2), the security agreement. The attorney will make sure those instruments are drafted and executed properly. Just make sure you have an attorney who is familiar with lending and real estate laws and practices, which should not be difficult to find in any city across the country.

The attorney should be somebody who understands what goals you are trying to achieve with your private lending investments. They want to know your risk tolerances. If your risk tolerance is a little bit less than aggressive, that's fine. Start slowly. You may be someone who, over time, likes to take a little bit more risk, or maybe you have buckets of money that have more risk. Your attorney will want to know that so they can help design and structure your documentation.

The attorney can also look out for pitfalls, such as issues with title, zoning, or the actual survey of a property. As you learn as you go, you'll also be able to make sure that you're not taking on too much risk.

The attorney will create documents to reflect anything that's unique about the structure of your deal. Remember, it's your opportunity as a private lender to create and structure the deals you want. You could be very creative with the borrower. You don't have to worry about making the documentation perfect because the attorney will take what you want and what you have agreed to with your borrower and put that into the legal language that's important for you. Don't let that catch you up.

There's always more potential opportunity in what we call unique deals, however, I don't encourage you to start with unique deals. I'll explain what those are later; stay very traditional and very basic at first. As you grow your expertise and your knowledge, you can start to get a little bit more complex, and there are opportunities with complexity, but also risk. Your attorney can help you make sure that you structure and document your deals according to your direction and what you desire.

TITLE COMPANY/ESCROW ATTORNEY

Some states use title companies, some use attorney escrows. You might hear the terms *escrow office, title company, title*

office, attorney title office, or *title closing office.* Essentially, they all mean the same thing, depending upon what state you're in. It's vital to use a title company, or a closing office, or an attorney in the state in which the property is located because you are lending money under the statutes of that state. You can't (or shouldn't) try to learn the regulations across fifty states. The title companies and attorneys in all states know what the statues and the rules are for their state.

You need a third party called either a title company, or it could be an attorney escrows. This third party handles the documentation and the funds to make the investment go through. They must be licensed. They're regulated to help execute the documentation that's provided by the attorneys. They take the funds, handle closing statements, wire money in and wire money out.

There have been instances, not too many, where we actually, in haste, wired money to the wrong title company for an investment deal. You'd say, "Oh, my gosh. You wire money out. How could you ever get that money back again?" In fact, all it took was one call from the third party to say to the other title company, "If you take a look at your account today, I wired some money. It was supposed to go to another title company." They sent it right back. That's why you have a third party. They make sure everything is done correctly to your instructions, as the lender, and they don't release your funds until everything is documented, so having a title company gives you that safeguard.

The title company acts on behalf of both the borrower and the lender, ensuring that the documents and the agreements that you've set up with that borrower are correct. They will execute, or close, the transaction, based on the contractual agreements you have. Your money will not be released until all the boxes are checked and all the directions are given.

Your team members let you do what you do best, and that's make deals. They let you network and find the opportunities. You negotiate, you structure the deal, and then you hand it off to these excellent team members who have expertise in taking the deal to fruition. That leaves you free to do what you do best. Don't get mired in the details.

INSURANCE AGENCY

The next team member that's very important is an insurance agency. Now, let's be clear here. As the lender, it's not your job to obtain insurance on the property on which you're lending money. That responsibility lies with the owner—the borrower. The borrower is always the one who's responsible for getting insurance, but you will be named as what we call a loss payee. You're the mortgagee in this case, a loss payee, so if there's ever a casualty to the property, if the property is damaged and it has to be repaired or fire burns it all the way down, your interest as a lender is listed on that policy, and you will be paid first. As the lender, you get paid before the owner gets any money.

I'll describe more about how that works in a subsequent chapter, but you have what's called an insurable interest. As a lender, you have an insurable interest, and the borrower, the owner of the property, is required at closing to provide an insurance binder that names you, the capital lender, as the insurable interest. Insurance lists you as the *mortgagee*, a term that means lender. It's part of the legalese that goes in a lot of documents. The insurance will never just write a check to the borrower. With you as the loss payee, the insurance company requires you to sign off on the proceeds of a claim first, so you're always protected. You're in what's called the chain of title, and no one can go around you to upset that.

It's the borrower's responsibility to get and pay for that insurance on the property. Make sure that the borrower is providing full-coverage insurance on the property, not just the amount you're lending, because as you'll find out a little bit later, we don't lend 100 percent of the value of a property. If a property is worth $100,000, you probably are only lending $75,000, but you still want that borrower to ensure the entire value of the property. You want that margin of safety in case the property is a total loss. You always get your principal, and anything that's left over goes to the borrower or the owner of the property. Natural disasters, floods, and fires don't happen often, but when they do, insurance is essential.

Sometimes you need an attorney to navigate the payout or proceeds, of an insurance claim. Again, this happens very infrequently, but if there ever is a situation when an insurance company doesn't want to pay on a claim, the attorney's there to make sure that that's settled appropriately for you. Insurance claims on real property probably take place less than 1 percent of the time, but that doesn't mean you want to go bare. Make sure your assets are protected, because if you're not covered that one time, you could experience a total loss of your money, and that's not the point of lending in real estate.

If you don't pay for the insurance, why do you need an agent? Occasionally, a borrower, for reasons I go into a little bit later, may go into default. If you follow the rules in these chapters, that won't happen very often, but if a borrower has a life calamity, an illness, maybe a disability, and cannot make the payments, then the insurance premiums also may go unpaid. In that situation you may need to have your own insurance agent step in and place what's called a force-placed policy.

A force-placed policy covers your interest and you get to

charge the cost back to the borrower. That's a claim that goes with your investment loan, so you'll get that money back, but sometimes you have to step in and make that happen. This policy protects you in the event that the borrower lets their policy lapse. Your attorney puts this into place upon your authorization, and now you have coverage.

CONTRACTOR OR INSPECTOR

A contractor or inspector can be one and the same. You want somebody who can inspect the property, since typically it's going to be rehabbed. You want to make sure that the property actually is being rehabilitated, the renovations are being made according to a schedule, that the borrower is doing what he said he would do. This approach is what we call "trust but verify." As you learn to lend money, you'll understand you don't just give the borrower all the money up front. You will typically give it to them in stages. I'll explain that later when we go over *draw schedules.*

You can do your own inspections if you feel qualified, but why spend your time doing that? Why not have a licensed inspector or a contractor that you approve of inspect that property? This is something that the borrower will pay for; you can set that in your term sheet. It's important to have the property inspected to make sure that the borrower is doing what he or she says they're going to do, and that your money's not being used in another project somewhere else. The way to make sure everything is happening correctly is for your contractor or inspector to verify what's happening with your money.

Make sure that this person is licensed in the state in which your property is located. If it's a contractor, you want to make sure that they have done this kind of work before, that they have experience inspecting or a contractor's experience so they know what to look for, and have a checklist of the rehabilitation that's been promised by your borrower.

The contractor or licensed inspector is a vital person, especially if you are loaning out of town or in another state. Our inspectors take pictures and video so we can actually see what's happening. You don't have to be there on-site, but you need somebody who is your eyes to keep everybody accountable. It's a great way to run a business.

Even though you might feel like you are lending money to good people, don't create the opportunity for somebody to maybe slip a little bit and not use the funds where they're supposed to use them. Even good people can fall into that temptation. Your borrower should never be offended and ask, "Well, why are you having me inspected?" That's just the way you run a business.

The contractor or the inspector is your eye on the ground. They make sure that the property that you're lending money on actually exists. Unfortunately, there are scam artists out there. They exist in every industry, not just real estate, and you have to be careful. People can seem like they have good character. They can act like they have a great track record; you still want someone to verify that the physical property that you're lending on exists.

A colleague of ours planned to lend money on a particular property, and when he sent an inspector by to verify the property, there was a shell: just the front of the building and nothing behind it. How would he know that if he hadn't sent someone there? Someone could easily take pictures of the front of the house and go, "Here's the house." It looked like it was all there, but behind it there was nothing. Nothing! That's why you want real eyes on the ground.

Make sure that the condition of the property is what the buyer represented to you. What level of rehabilitation does it need? Does it need full rehabilitation including all the mechanicals, structure, foundation, and roof, or is it just a light cosmetic job of paint, carpet, and flooring? Your contractor or inspector can go look at the property before you commit to make sure you're lending on what you believe you're lending on.

Then they'll confirm the rehab's being done as it was agreed upon in the contract, and that it's on schedule. If there are issues, such as someone takes a bit longer, that's not an issue as long as it's all verified and communicated, which is why you want that inspector. You may have a borrower who says, "We were trying to put a new roof on the property, and we had a rain delay." Those are real-life situations, and you can be flexible, but your flexibility has to be connected to facts that can be documented so you don't let anybody just run with excuses. Before you release the next round of funds from your loan, make sure they have completed what they said they were going to do. That's what that contractor or inspector will do for you.

ACCOUNTANT

You need an accountant. You might tell yourself that learning QuickBooks and doing it all yourself is easy, and you might save a little money. But why are you investing your time in activities that do not generate revenue? Just be sure someone is taking care of the real estate and financial side of the transactions. It's not as simple as keeping track of expenses, like a personal checking account. This work involves various aspects of accountability, such as making sure your CPA has information about your taxes, and you are tuned into your return on investment. If you don't have somebody who's good with spreadsheets giving you updates from time to time, how will you know if your money is working for you? Is it working the way you want it to?

People who are good with numbers can do this so easily. There's no reason at all why you can't hire a virtual bookkeeper to help you with the kind of information that you need. Look for an organized person, someone who's detail oriented who can help you track your funds. You can give them access to your bank accounts, not to perform transactions, but to review your accounts so they can look at money going out, funding, and money coming back in. If you're not a detailed person or you want to work on the big picture, orchestrating deals, you need that person on your team.

They don't have to have high-end bookkeeping skills. If they have modest skills, they can do what you need done for private lending. Someone who has a good attitude, good work ethic, and the right profile can be trained. You can hire somebody who can undertake virtual training, and start logging in the financials of the investments you're making.

It's not a bad idea for you to track some of your own investments at first. When you have one, two, three, maybe a small handful of private lending deals in place, track those so you can see what the numbers look like, then turn that over to someone who can really help you scale this up. Knowing your numbers allows you to know all the nuances of how your lending works, how money goes out, money comes back in, and how it's being tracked. It also allows you to provide more accurate training before you delegate more of your services and the fiduciary aspects of your own private capital lending.

How do you find these team members? The most important source is your own professional and personal networks. Whenever we're looking for somebody we need to add to our team—part-time, virtual, or full-time person—the first place we go to is our network. We ask other people who are involved in real estate, "Who do you use? Who do you know?" Start with your own network. Outside of that, you can go to referrals, so ask other people. If they don't know somebody, ask, "Who do you know that might know somebody else who could provide the expertise we need?"

Real estate investment groups are a great place for this.

Consider local real estate investment association groups that meet regularly in most mid- to larger-sized metropolitan areas. Join online communities like Facebook groups about real estate investing in a local community. See what people are talking about. It's a great place to ask for referrals for any of the team members you might need.

How do you go about qualifying a team member? Once you have a referral or a candidate, whether it's the attorney, the CPA, the bookkeeper, the contractor, or the inspector, always talk to people for whom they've already provided services. Get a list of people they are currently working with or have worked with in the past. Call those people and say, "How was it working with Matt Stone? How was it working with Mary Smith? Did they give you prompt service? Was it the kind of service you needed?" Ask the person to show you the kind of projects that they've worked on. See if the detail is what you want. Do you communicate well with them? Do you have good rapport with them?

If you need the person to do a lot of your financials and have access to your accounts, conduct a background check. Have them step into that role slowly. Don't hand over too much access to your confidential information until you have a chance to see how a person's working out. Ask them how long they've been doing the kind of work you're hiring for, their training, and their experience level.

There are different aspects to real estate: the retail side and the investor side. There are a few companies that deal with both sides well, but oftentimes, you want to look for an investor-friendly CPA, an investor-friendly management company, and an investor-friendly title company. They're used to working at our pace and on more creative deals. That's the kind of person or company you're looking to work with.

How many other real estate investors are currently clients with them? What percentage of their business incorporates using investors' money and investors' transactions? Have they had any negative experiences with other investors? Is there a particular type of transaction they don't like to do? Are there certain types of documents that they don't like to do? Just getting involved and asking them the right questions is the biggest thing you can do.

If you are investing in your local area and you're looking for title companies, go to their office and meet with them. Get to know them and tell them about yourself and what you do. We do a lot of business in other states and sometimes fly to meet the people there who are boots on the ground. That's not required when you're first getting started, but when you can do that, it makes such a difference to have that real communication. That connection is a big part of how you scale your business and how you're able to do more deals with more frequency and with much more ease.

CHAPTER 15

IMPORTANCE OF DUE DILIGENCE

What is this thing called *due diligence*? In the real estate investment world, it means investigating and checking out all aspects of something or someone.

We want to determine what's real, versus what's claimed, versus what's assumed. In real estate, many times you'll be given what's called a *pro forma*. Pro forma means a projection of how this investment should go, the time frame, and your projected return on investment. Pro formas are fine as a starting point, but it's your job to dig deep and make sure you verify the facts, the nature, and the assumptions being made as a part of your potential investment deal. That's doing due diligence.

Researching the Investment

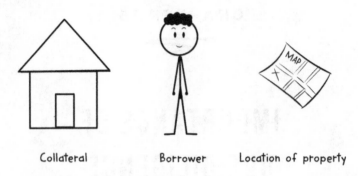

Collateral   Borrower   Location of property

As a private lender you will conduct research on three main elements of this particular investment deal.

The first is the property, also known as the collateral. Your real estate investment lending deal is secured by the property via the promissory note and the security agreement. The property is part of mitigating your risk, so you want to make sure you understand the property your money is being invested against. What does the property look like? Is it a house, is it an apartment, is it broken down, is it in a good neighborhood, is it in a bad neighborhood?

You also want to know the background of your borrower. If you're getting started with private lending, you can meet somebody at a real estate association meeting, through a network, or through professional associations. Undoubtedly somebody's going to say, "Hey, John, I've got a great deal for you. I'm rehabbing a house over on North Street. I need some capital. Would you like to be my private lender?" Before investing, you must do background work on this potential borrower. What's his or her track record? What kinds of deals have they done, and what's their general character like?

Understand the area where the property is located. You might not think that's important, but it is. What's the economic basis of the neighborhood? What does the neighborhood look like? Invest your capital in a property that's in a neighborhood where you wouldn't mind living. That doesn't mean it has to be the house you live in, but the neighborhood should be safe, a place where you'd let a family member (one that you like!) live in or walk down the street at 8:00 on a Saturday evening. If it's too risky for that, then you're probably in the wrong area. You want to be in an area where there are good demographics, good schools and churches, access to jobs, freeways, and shopping. You want neighborhoods that are established, not necessarily new subdivisions where economic change might cause a total change there. You want something that has a track record.

DUE DILIGENCE

There are a number of ways to conduct due diligence. Maybe you want to invest your capital with a borrower who's out of town or out of state. Well, where would you start? Get on the phone. Call realtors and management companies and find out what the area is like. What do properties rent for, what are they selling for, what's the activity in the marketplace? You also should talk to other people who have done business with your potential borrower. The borrower should be very willing to give you names of people they do business with, who have lent money to them, who have done contract jobs for them. Call title companies and banks, too.

Call a good handful—three, four, even six—until you find that the information you get back is consistent. "Yes, Matt Stone does what he says he's going to do. If there's an issue, he always communicates. He never leaves me holding the bag or wondering what's happening next." That's what you're looking for. You want consistency in someone's track record.

GO ONLINE

Google's a great resource; you can find out all kinds of things about people. Do they have any legal judgments against them, any lawsuits, any zoning issues, any issues with the community or the Board of Realtors? You can go to Facebook profiles and get an idea about the person's character and who they hang around with. People don't realize the opportunities available to do some of their own online research. You also can hire someone to do this, people who are really good at research, if you want to go further and deeper.

PERSONAL INTERVIEWS

Think of what you are doing like a job interview. Request the borrowers' resume, showing all of the projects they've done, transaction history, and credit report, as well as business references and personal references. This should not be a surprise request for your borrowers. They should have this ready to present. If they don't have any of it, or don't want to share it, you have no business considering investing with them. Once you have all of this information, you can start your interview process.

Whenever possible, make this a face-to-face meeting with your borrower. You should get to know them and not just what they know about the specific real estate investment. What's their background? Where did they come from? Have they always been in real estate or have they changed focus recently? Do they have a background in construction? Have they run a business before, or is this their first time? What's their financial capacity? Do they have a grasp of numbers? We talked about your team—what's their team like?

Meet the potential borrower where he or she lives. Meet the family, the spouse and the kids. You want to see how they relate. You want to see how they communicate and what kind of respect exists in the relationships. You want to be there when they meet with their team to see what their meetings look like. See how they talk about the projects they're doing and how they are going. Who's there? Who's in charge? What does the leadership look like? What is the culture like? These are very important things, and you can't see this just by talking one-on-one. You have to see your potential borrowers in their work environment, and with whom they do business and how they communicate. Go with them to their other projects and see how they communicate with tenants and workmen.

Look for someone who has a rhythm, they're meeting on a regular basis, they're doing regular deal flow every month. Ask if you can ride around and see how they handle any problems that arise, or ask them what issues they've had and how they dealt with them. If everything were easy in life, we wouldn't need to look for opportunities, would we? Solving problems is a key, but doing it with other people who know how to solve those problems is one of the things that make a huge difference, and it's where the opportunities are. Bottom line, you want someone who will respect your money and treat the project like a business.

Make sure that you assess their level of experience with renovating and borrowing. It's important. How many deals have they done? Are you going to work with someone who's relatively new or has a track record? Look at their settlement statement (closing documents) from deals that they've done, from when they bought the property to when they sold it. Check the time frame. These settlement statements are in their files, and they can easily produce them. If they can't, that's a big red flag. Ask for at least a half a dozen from the last six to nine months. You want to see how many projects they're doing and the time periods.

If there's something that falls out of the normal range, like one property took nine months to finish and the other ones are typically taking four or five or six, ask, "What was the deal on the property on Elm Street?" Listen to the story. You're always looking for stories to learn more and verify or disprove what you think is going on. A delay doesn't mean that there's a problem with the borrower. If there's a reliable story about Elm Street, the deal still got done, and they communicated well with their lender, it's probably good. That's what you're looking for. You're looking for anomalies, then verifying why the anomalies took place.

HISTORY OF PROFIT

See how much profit they made. You want to lend money to people who make money, right? You want to make sure they have a good profit. If they're razor thin on their profit or they lose money on some deals, they're probably not a person you want to do business with because they have some issues somewhere, right? Check out where they are having issues: with the purchase price or the selling price. If one particular property shows up with negligible profit margin, ask, "What happened on this one?" Is there a reliable story? Does it make sense? Was there a real issue that couldn't be ascertained on the front end? The fact that they still went through and did the deal and took their marginal profit and called it good, that's all right.

TIMELINES

Look at their timelines. How long is it taking them to get through a project with their deals? How many deals are they doing at once? How many do they have in the pipeline? Are they capable of managing that number of deals? Get a list of their subcontractors, the plumbers, the electricians, the roofers, and ask them, "Matt Stone, does he pay you on time? Do you ever have any issues? Does he delay payments? Does he ever call you and then he's not ready for you?" You're looking for consistency and the borrower's ability to manage a project. As a lender, make sure that they have that business acumen.

REFERENCES

Talk to other people who have been lending money to this borrower. Again, get half a dozen people who are doing business with them now and people who have done business in the past. Your aim is to lend to people who have good character, not a bunch of partnership or business breakups because they couldn't communicate. Look for long-term relationships. Your borrowers should be people who know how to deal with people, who can solve problems. They are where opportunities come from, so look for that in a borrower. Make sure their communication is always consistent and accurate with their vendors. That goes for the subcontractors, the title companies, and the attorneys. Check around. Does this person do what they say they're going to do? Are they on time? Do they ever have issues with their buyers or their renters or people they're buying from? I'm always keeping my ears tuned to that kind of thing because we want to deal with people who have figured it out, who know how to run a business, and how to manage and talk to people.

EXTENSIONS

Does the borrower need an extension? Again, there's nothing wrong with someone needing an extension. Most of our lending agreements include an opportunity to extend the loan terms if the borrower needs more time. But we want to document why. Is it justified, or are they just being sloppy? It could be that they need more time because of a market condition. Sometimes there's a purchase contract and, by no fault of your borrower, the buyer couldn't get funding. The loan didn't go through, the underwriting didn't pass, so they have to start over. That stuff happens. That's legitimate, and we'll do an extension. You can negotiate your extensions. You can waive a fee for the first extension, for instance, and then charge an extension fee later if you need to. You can actually add profit to your lending if that makes sense for the market and the person you're doing business with. You're the one who has the money; you get to set a certain number of the rules and criteria.

PAYMENTS

Did the borrower make their payments on time? If there was a delay or need for an extension, did they communicate that in advance? You want people who communicate. You don't want to chase people down and find out why your investment is not being paid on time. When you're first starting with somebody new, run a credit report. You need to see what their trade history is with all of their other accounts:

mortgage, loans, auto, and utility accounts. A credit report will show that. A good borrower will not flinch when you ask them for that. If they do flinch, they're probably somebody you don't want to do business with.

Don't skip this step with your friends. Run a credit report on them also. There could be something there that you don't know about, and it's better to find out now and decide either to do business or not do business, than to run into a problem later. That's how friendships are broken up. Sometimes friends should just be friends and you shouldn't do business with them. You have to make that decision, but you can only do it when you have all of the information that comes from a credit check.

TITLE SEARCH

Once you've received a list of past projects from the borrower, ask the title company to conduct title searches. Research the actual property to make sure the borrower actually owns it. Also check the title on past and pending projects. Make sure the properties have what we call a clean or clear title, meaning there are no judgments against it and the person who they're buying it from can actually convey, or give, the title to them. That's why the title company or attorney escrow is on your team. That title search will confirm that the title on the current project is good and valid—which also means your lender position, your lien position, your security agreement are also valid and good, and there are no offsets, which would be someone else's claim against your position.

PROPERTY VALUATION

Make sure you understand the valuation of the property. Most of the properties you will lend money against are an opportunity for the wholesale contractor or rehabber to pick them up at a discount, or wholesale, value. When they acquire the property, it generally is not in tip-top shape. That's where the opportunity is. It will need some work. You want to know what this property really is worth today, and what the property is going to be worth when the scheduled renovations are done. That's what's called after-repaired value, or ARV. When the property is renovated to the specifications in your contract and your agreement with the borrower, what's that property going to be worth? What's it worth today, right now, on a quick-sale basis? That determines how much money you want to invest in this deal to keep you in a safe position.

BETTER BUSINESS BUREAU

Further due diligence can also involve looking at the Better Business Bureau. Many business people cite the Better Business Bureau as one of their affiliations so that they can prove they have a track record and show when there are issues, they've taken care of their customers. You're looking for all of those aspects. That's part of your due diligence.

INVESTOR-FRIENDLY LOCATIONS

Look at the state and city or municipality in which your property is located. Some states are more business or investor friendly, and some are not so friendly. Some are more consumer oriented. If you're the investor, you want to be in a state that typically provides a good safety net, or at least stands up for the interests of the investor. Not that you want them to be anti-consumer—it's important there's a balance. California, for instance, is a state where laws favor consumers, almost to the degree of an entitlement or a victim mentality. If you choose to do business there, create more of a margin of safety so if you do get entangled in situations with litigation or small claims court, you have some reserves. In other words, don't sink all your money in the deal. Have some cash to take care of a problem, should one come up.

LOCAL LAWS

If you're going to invest outside of your own state, call the title company attorney, or call the escrow attorney, or call a general real estate agent. Ask them, "Tell me a little bit about the laws in your state, especially from a real estate standpoint as a private lender. What do I need to know?

What's different about the laws in your state that wouldn't necessarily be conventional with other states?" That's a great question to ask, and the title company attorney should be glad to spend a few minutes with you explaining the particular nuances of investing in that state or locale.

Review documents carefully with your attorney. That's why you have an attorney on your team. When there's something specific to that state you haven't seen before, the attorney will explain it: "Well, this is why we use this document, because in this state we need this. It covers you, it protects you, and it is a disclosure form to make sure that we comply with all the lending laws in that particular state." Don't assume that just because you do business in one state and get comfortable there, the same laws will pertain across the board. Have an attorney, who's familiar with the laws and statutes in each state you lend in, make sure you're in compliance and will not ever face what we call an offset or counterclaim, should something arise against your loan. You want to make sure your documents and your protocols are all in line, so that no one can ever say that you didn't follow proper procedures and, therefore, put your investment capital at risk.

Again, you can remove a lot of those issues or risks just by doing your due diligence on the front end. The good news is we're lending money to businesses, not consumers. Consumer loans have a lot more issues and a different lending environment, so we stay away from that in our private lending business.

ADDITIONAL GEOGRAPHIC CONSIDERATIONS

Know the economic climate of the state. In other words, there are states where the economic climate is stronger, where it's a lower tax state so that the economy does better. Look for states where the economy's more robust, because a downturn can put your capital at risk. Invest in an environment that you feel comfortable with, and be sure you've accounted for potential risk if you are investing in states where it might be a little bit more hazardous. Look for growth sectors, areas where business is coming in, where the environment and the political climate are welcoming to new business and not creating a lot of barriers to entry. With new businesses comes more people, and more people means you have a more robust housing market to make your value stand and stay strong for your capital investment.

POPULATION GROWTH

Are people moving more into the state or are they moving out of the state? Here's a little trick. Call the local U-Haul dealer and ask, "How much is it to rent a U-Haul to leave the state, and how much to bring one back in?" That pricing will tell you whether people are moving in or out. If there are a lot of U-Hauls coming into the state, that's a good thing. If a lot of them are going out the other way, that's probably not so good.

Look at your own state's economic growth and decide if you're in a geographic environment where the price points of the capital you want to invest make sense. (I'll talk a little bit more about price points later.) You very well could decide to invest in your own state. If you like all the other dynamics of some of the due diligence we talked about, your own state may be a good place. As I mentioned earlier, the flyover states are steady locations. The East Coast, West Coast—Florida, California, Nevada, Arizona—are typically states that have a relatively large amount of volatility. When the market's up, those markets tend to climb rapidly and escalate in price point. Not to say that you can't make money in those markets, but that's really more of a hands-on situation. You have to deal with people who have a finger on the pulse of those markets, and it's a little bit more speculative.

If you're getting started with real estate private lending, we recommend you stick to more nonvolatile markets, which would be Midwestern states, or Texas, Oklahoma, Indiana, Ohio, or Alabama, just to name a few where there's not a lot of volatility. As you become more astute in your investing and you find some good partners in areas that are more volatile, there are opportunities there. But don't start in the volatile markets.

SURVEY THE NEIGHBORHOOD

Once you're in that geographic area, survey the neighborhood. Look around and ask, "Well, what do the other houses look like in the neighborhood?" Are they all pretty well taken care of? Does it look like it's more of an owner-occupied area, or does it look like this is a rental neighborhood? (If it's rental, it's probably not an area you want to invest in.) Your neighborhood does not have to be perfect. It can be an area that's being gentrified, but you want to make sure there's a positive trend, that there's a pride of ownership. If there are rental properties, make sure they're being taken care of. Don't go into an area where things are kind of run down and not looking good, because you may, in a worst-case scenario, end up owning that house and need to divest yourself of it. You want to be in an area where you feel comfortable investing, where you are confident you can get your money back out.

Stability, in the form of churches, shopping areas and schools, demonstrates the economic base, and creates greater interest in property and higher valuations. They remain stable or they rise with the market, versus declining because nobody wants to go there. There might be some really great opportunities, some very discounted prices that your wholesale or joint venture partners can get in those areas. But do you really want to be a part of that? You have to look with discernment before you jump in.

RISK TOLERANCE

Doing your due diligence properly helps you align your investment venture with your risk tolerance. Many times, a husband and wife who are investing together need to be in concert, and oftentimes one or the other is more conservative. If you're starting where one of you has a little more fear, a little more anxiety, mitigate your risk. Go into a safe deal. Don't go for some high-yield return; go for a nice 6 percent, 7 percent, 8 percent return on your money with a rock-solid deal. Get that down. Do a few of those deals.

Chasing the Yield

CHASING THE YIELD

What we call chasing yield—trying to get the highest return on your money—is a fool's game, because you can only do that so many times before you get burned. Here and there you might get a really good deal because there's a great profit opportunity with a person you work with. That's awesome when that happens, but don't set the bar so high that you're chasing yield and going after riskier deals. To get a higher yield on your money, you have to take a little bit more risk. Sometimes that's okay, but you have to know what you're doing.

TYPE OF PROPERTY

Identify what type of projects you will fund. Some rehabs are "all in"—the property needs just about everything. It might need some foundation work, it might need exterior stucco or brick work, it might need a new roof and new mechanicals: air conditioning, water heater, furnace. There's nothing wrong with that. Just know what you're getting into, and make sure the person to whom you're lending money has done those kinds of deals. If they're relatively new and don't have a lot of experience, it's probably not something you want to wade into, because what's likely to happen? They're going to come back to you and say, "Gee, I underestimated the bid on this job. I need more money." That's the last thing you want to hear, because that means you're putting more money into a deal that's already running short on margin.

CAPITAL LIMITS

Some deals will need more money, but make sure you work

with people who have a strong track record. People with good track records sometimes need more money, but they have to show their request is an exception and not the norm. They shouldn't be someone who just gets into a deal and need more money to keep them going.

What's the maximum amount of capital that you want to put into any one deal? Let's say you have $100,000 to invest. Do you want to put all $100,000 into one deal, or might it be smarter to break it up and do 33 percent, 33 percent, and 33 percent, or some combination? You don't want all your eggs in one basket, and you get more experience by spreading your money around. Rather than putting that money in one deal, put it in two or three deals. Get the money working, get the money back, and go on to the next deal. That's how you start building capital momentum.

INVESTMENT TO VALUE LIMITS

What's the maximum investment to value ratio you should seek in one deal? Investment to value (ITV) means the amount of your capital you are putting in relative to the value of the property. Let me give you an example. Let's say that the value of the property on a wholesale basis today is $60,000, and you've verified that through realtors or comparable sale data. Say your borrower buys that property for $50,000, so they're getting it at a little bit of a discount. They're going to put another $25,000 into the property to bring it up to the value they want before they take it to market, where they'll either sell it or rent it.

So now we have $50,000, plus $25,000 in rehab, for a total of $75,000. The after-repaired value can be estimated by looking at comparable sale values of properties that are in good condition, rehabbed in that neighborhood. Let's say the after-repaired value is $100,000. Now you're contemplating investing a total of $75,000 of your capital against a property that when it's completed will be worth $100,000. That's what we call a 75 percent investment to value ratio, or ITV. Your investment of $75,000 is 75 percent of the total value of the after-repaired value. That's a pretty safe ratio. As a lender, you shouldn't go higher than 80 percent, and that's only with a top-tier property in an area that's very active. We try to stay around 75 percent, or even lower, in our ITV ratio. If you have to step in and foreclose on the property, you have some to cover your costs and make a profit when you resell (more on this later on).

That's a way you can mitigate risk. Maybe for your first deal you don't want to go above 50 or 55 percent investment to value. That's fine. You may have to look a little bit harder for a borrower who will do that, but someone who likes you and knows that you will do deals on an ongoing basis will probably let you in on a deal with a lower investment to value to get you started, so that you feel comfortable with your first deals.

This is about relationship building. It's a two-way street. Working together, building those relationships, is how all this works. Don't ever be afraid to let someone know your risk tolerance.

RISK TOLERANCE

As I said, you can start with that lower investment to value. Also, you can lend your money on properties that need a lighter, more cosmetic rehab: floor, carpet, painting, maybe some fixtures, nothing major, so that your borrower doesn't get in over their head and have to ask you for more money. It's okay to do harder or more extensive rehabs with borrowers who have that track record. If you want to go in and participate in those deals when you have a little more experience, go for it.

The other advantage with smaller projects is they're going to finish quickly. If you're looking at a time frame where you're doing a shorter lending deal—six months, maybe eight, nine months at most—you get your money back sooner. That's a good thing when you want to see how this program works. You put your money out, and you're on pins and needles for a few weeks. You're thinking, "I hope this works, I hope this works." Once you get that money back, you can breathe. You think, "Wow, when's the next one?"

At some point, you'll say, "Well, it's a lot of work to have to put my money back out again. Every time I've got to do the due diligence all over again, at least on the property, if not the borrower." Yes, you do. At some point, you're going to want to do deals that are for a longer term, and I'll explain how those work. To get started, just get your money working for you on short deals.

The type of property you invest your capital in is also very, very important. I recommend that new lenders stick with single-family houses. Why? Single-family houses are easy to identify, they're easy to classify, they're easy to evaluate, they're easy to inspect, and they're easy to do due diligence on. Bedrooms, bathrooms, kitchens, maybe a garage or a carport. It isn't that complicated, right? It's not hard to do. It doesn't cost you a lot of time or a lot of money to have someone else help you do the due diligence. When you start climbing the ladder to more complex lending, there will be more moving parts. You will need a greater degree of due diligence and underwriting, which you're going to have to learn to do yourself or by relying on that great team you're building. So start with single family, because it's safer, with a lower investment, so you can be more diversified.

Another note about "neighborhood normal": stay away from what we call unique property. A unique property doesn't fit within the norm of a neighborhood. We like "bread-and-butter neighborhoods," where there's a whole subdivision of houses all built about the same time, but not necessarily by the same builder. They have similar square footage and layouts. They're either ranch style, or maybe they're two storied, depending on the locale, but they're all about the same. Don't invest money in the outlier. The outlier could be some really cool property in some neat, upcoming area, but what if something happens with that property? Only a limited number of buyers will want that, which could put you in a bind. Unique property means someone likes it because it has some artistic flavor. That's great, but probably not where you want to be lending your money. Stay with bread-and-butter stuff, even though you personally might like the cool stuff.

Remember, this is about making money. If you want to play and be creative, have separate money on the side for that. Don't put your hard-to-work money in something that's unique and could become a problem if the market changes, or if the creativity of the borrower didn't quite work out, if they couldn't rent it or sell it the way they expected. When you stay with conformity, you know that there will be a buyer or a renter for that property, because that's what the majority is looking for. That's what keeps you safe and makes it easy for you.

Start by working with experienced borrowers. That may seem hard, because you say, "Well, experienced buyers don't need me." Here's the truth: experienced borrowers are always looking for additional streams of lending capital because they never want to be tied to one person or one source of money. If you're a person of character and you express an interest and you build that relationship, an experienced borrower will say, "You know what? I like you. I know you haven't done a lot of this, but it sounds like if we can make this work together, we can do a lot of deals." That's what you're looking for. That experienced borrower will keep you safe. The tendency is for new lenders to connect with new rehabbers or new joint venture partners. Everyone on the team may be new at the game. They tell themselves, "Well, we'll partner up because we kind of speak the same language. We both don't know what we're doing, so it should be a marriage made in heaven, right?" Well, it's not. It's probably the worst thing you can do.

It's better for an experienced private lender to joint venture with an inexperienced borrower, because that lender can be more of a mentor. The other way around, you want an experienced borrower to borrow from you the first time that you're lending money, because they can actually walk you through it and show you the things I'm talking about here. They should be able to show you all the due diligence without you even having to ask. They'll show you all the aspects of what they're setting up to do, how they'll build the property out, how they'll renovate it, and the schedule. They should provide all of it for you. It's a great opportunity.

On those first deals with an experienced borrower, don't go

for top yield. Lend your money at a lower yield. Tell them, "I'll do the first deals with you at 6 percent." It's not about that return, it's about returning your principal and having consistency with return and building relationships. Over time, you can meet in the middle and you can up your yield a little bit.

CO-LEND PARTNER

You don't always have to put all of your own money into a lending deal. Say there's a deal that has an opportunity to lend $100,000 and you have $50,000 in one of your accounts ready to go. If you have a friend who also has $50,000, two of you, even three of you if you're good friends, can invest together to make one good, solid loan. If there's someone who you think you would like to do that with, you need to do a little vetting of him or her, right? You want to make sure that they have the same attitude, risk tolerance, and at least some trust and some education in what you're doing with private lending. They might invest in a deal that's going to go six, eight, nine, or twelve months, and then three months later say, "Hey, I need my money back out." It doesn't work that way. You've got to have someone who's on the same page with you.

Ask them questions about their motivation. Why do they want to do private lending? What do they know about it? Is it just something they've heard you talk about? Are they only looking to make quick money? Remember, nothing in life is sustainable if it's always about the quick return, the quick home run. If they think they will hit a home run lending with you, they're probably not the right person. Not everybody's cut out to be a lender. They might be a Nervous Nellie. They might want to check on the property every day, or call the borrower and ask them how it's going. Your borrowers don't want that micromanagement. You want someone who's probably run a business, so they have that business acumen, they're savvier in business, and they understand finances. They understand there are always some risks in life and how to mitigate risks, so they won't be so nervous.

What's their background? Have they invested in real estate or done any lending before? What experience do they have with any kind of financing? Do they have decision-making experience because they've run a business, or are in a position in a company where they make a lot of decisions? In other words, do they have control over what they do? Do they know how to make decisions with confidence, and can they make good decisions when they do research and with critical thinking? If you dig a little, you might find out they have a history of suing everybody they do business with. That's probably not someone you want to partner with, so be diligent about researching them.

CHAPTER 16

WORKING WITH BORROWERS AND LENDERS

Before lending, you have to assess the quality of the borrower. I wrote about that earlier; now we'll go deeper.

There are certain characteristics you want to see in a borrower. It's important that they are a business owner. They should be experienced at running their processes of rehabbing properties, and finding properties should be their primary business. They should have people on their team and have created a culture and processes that make their systems work.

It's important that they are familiar with making decisions as a business leader. They have experience and understand business and financial risks. As I mentioned before, because you are a new lender, you don't want a new borrower. You want an experienced borrower, otherwise you will be handling more issues than you want. They should show you statements from their prior projects—closing statements that demonstrate time frame and the amount of profit they made.

WHERE TO FIND YOUR BORROWERS

Finding Borrowers

Your Network

Referrals

Real Estate Association Groups

Online Discussion Groups

Facebook Lending Groups

It all starts with your network. I described in the first few chapters of this section of the book the inefficiency of the private lending arena. That inefficiency is an opportunity. It is where you enter and create a network. Our network has been one of the most important factors in our business and our lives. It gives us access to opportunities, deal flow, and borrowers with whom we can create amazing success and profit. It's a win-win-win across the board. We all profit when we work together, but that has to be done with the right people.

One of our colleagues calls his network his "net worth," and it's so true. The relationship capital you develop and maintain is one of the key ingredients for getting anywhere in life, and that's no different in private lending and real estate.

Be a part of a different group, online or offline. Go to association meetings where they have education about real estate where real estate investors typically hang out. They network, they mingle. Find out who's who, and who's talking about the deals they're doing. See who's respected in that group and talk to them. Take them out to lunch. Take them for coffee. Don't be afraid to ask questions. Just because you're bringing the capital into the deal doesn't mean you have to know everything. Be frank with people and say, "I'm getting started doing this. I want to learn how to do it. I want to do it with people who have experience." At the same time let them know who you have lined up on your team—the attorney, title company, inspector, etc.—and that you know enough about investing that you're going to have verifications along the way. Be confident enough, and humble enough, to ask questions. People love to talk about themselves and their successes. Encourage them!

Referrals are always the best way to find team members or borrowers, so ask around. Who are the people who have a good track record, who've been doing this for a while, who have the respect of the group? Ask people. Ask, ask, and ask. The real estate association groups meet locally and many times they have an online forum or community. Join those.

Get online. Get connected with our REWW community with thousands of other investors. See what people are talking about. Don't be afraid to ask your questions there, either. It's a great place to learn and get educated. Look for other real estate discussion groups and blogs. Not only is this a great way to get more education, it also gives you access to people. Garner visibility and information by commenting and asking questions on online articles. Check out real estate group pages on Facebook. If the page is a solid resource, they will share articles, videos, and live discussions. See who else has liked and consistently contributes to the page. If you are able to write a post, share links to interesting articles with your comments. Remember that when you interact with every group, live or online, you are doing your best to add value and share information, not just "taking" by only asking questions.

You will also find out, either online or offline, who within those communities likes to mentor. There are people in every group who've had success and like to give back. They like to help people. Seek them out. Don't take advantage of them; buy them lunch or dinner, then ask for information. They will be one of your best resources for lining you up with the right people.

While you are connecting with people, it's critical to post or speak in specifics. So, when you talk about lending money, be clear about what you are looking for. What size investments are you looking to make? What price points, what market, what area or geographic area? Are you looking for light rehab or are you willing to go into harder, extensive rehab? Are you looking to lend long term or short term? Those are some of the general criteria to establish so people who might want to do business with you know whether there is a potential fit. That way you're not wasting your time or theirs.

Build relationships organically through networking. It's one-on-one. It's talking to people. It's hearing people speak about what they do. Create conversations in person and explore those leads. This takes longer, but the work on the front end is so important, so worthwhile. Don't be hasty. We know you're excited about wanting to lend money. It's fun. Once you get started, you'll get hooked on it, as we have been for so many years, but take the time to build the infrastructure. Build your foundation—do it the right way. Don't cut corners and you'll be so much happier not making a mistake early on and then wishing you hadn't started, or heard your spouse say, "See, I told you so, you shouldn't have done this." Private lending is such an amazing opportunity and a great investment; it's not worth trying to get the instant gratification and quick money. It's too valuable to rush.

THE AMAZING WORLD OF ARBITRAGE

What is arbitrage? Arbitrage is simply the process of addressing the inefficiencies in a market. When I started working in our family business, I used arbitrage to wholesale items in the grocery industry. I was able to address the inefficiencies by looking at how that industry traditionally operated. A manufacturer of an item, any item, was selling it at a discount and a retailer bought that item, added a markup and resold it for a profit, just down the road from the manufacturer. They created an opportunity.

When I stepped into the process, I used the arbitrage method. I bought the items at the discounted price, shipped them across town, and sold to the retailer at an even lower price than the retailer was accustomed to paying the manufacturer, but high enough where I was making a profit.

Another great example of arbitrage is what the banks do with your money. I explained this earlier, and it's worth repeating. The banks borrow money from the deposits you make and they proudly pay you a measly .1 percent, or .5 percent. Then they turn around and lend it out to the world for a mortgage at 4, 5, 6, 7, or even 8 percent. The bank does not own your money. It's still your money. The bank is a middleman. They relend the money to other businesses, or real estate, or business expansion, or lines of credit, or for equipment at a higher rate. The spread—the difference in the market—is arbitrage. They didn't manufacture anything, they didn't make anything, they just added a markup on the other end of their business model. They have created a spread because the market is terribly inefficient. You haven't effectively figured out a way to go and loan that money directly out, nor are you in a position to do it. So they make their money in between. They make money off of other people's money.

You can do the same thing. Here's how it works: you simply pay a lower rate of interest within your network than you get from your borrowers because you have access to deal flow. Let me give you an example. Say you know people who have always wanted to invest in real estate but don't want to be a landlord or rehabber. They are frustrated with the low interest they are earning on their certificates of deposit, stocks and bonds, and money market accounts. Many of them actually like the idea of lending money because of the safety and the yield potential. They like that, but they don't have the time to build a network, learn about how to be a private lender or perform due diligence on borrowers. It's not their thing; they don't have the passion for it you do.

They want to invest their money through you. You have access to deals, you know the right people, you've learned the mechanics and nuances and how to do due diligence. Let's say you're experienced enough that you're lending money at 10 percent or above. You may very well have a colleague, a social acquaintance, who would be glad to see their money secured by specific collateral at say, 6 percent. You take the 4 percent spread between 6 percent and 10 percent. You make money on their money. You don't have to have all of your money in a deal. You could put some of your money in, but the key thing is you can make money on their deal.

Using arbitrage extends your lending abilities to help others. We all run out of money at some point. We have deal flow access; we have people who want to borrow money. At some point, we've invested all of our money. It's all out there—it's deployed. That's a good thing because your money is working for you. If you have a circle of people—it doesn't need to be many, it could be two or three people who start to build up a track record with you—you could have access to other people's money. And a good place for that, which I'll talk about a bit later too, is people's retirement accounts, especially self-directed individual retirement accounts, like traditional IRA or Roth IRA. It could be someone's business 401(k) if they have the ability to self-direct it, and they could lend money into the deal so that you have access to it.

An investor currently makes the typical 1 percent or less

on their money at the bank, and they'd love to be able to make more. You could say to them, "I can get you four, five, or six times what you make in the bank, and it's a secured loan. Does that sound interesting to you?" You should be able, on the back of a napkin, to show them how it works. You can learn to do this very easily; it doesn't need to be a fancy presentation. It's a simple process, and once you learn how it works, you can explain it very well.

At the same time, you're able to loan the money to your joint venture borrower at a typical 12 percent rate. So you're borrowing money from your friend at 6 percent and lending it at 12; you have a spread or an arbitrage difference of 6 percent. You keep that difference, in this case, without investing any of your own money. Your co-lender is making 6 percent on their money, and you're making 6 percent on the whole deal. You're each making money on the same investment.

You're acting as a bank, except in this case by doing it on an individual basis, small scale, you can do this without regulation and without a license. Before you start, run your plan by an attorney so you don't get into any issues, ever, with securities laws. If you keep your work small, and you're not out advertising for other people's money, you can do this kind of lending safely. But always have your attorney verify what you're doing to make sure that he or she feels like you're complying with the laws in that state.

Making money on other people's money, helping them at the same time you're making money, and helping the local economy by investing money on Main Street instead of Wall Street, is a great thing for everybody. Again, it's a win-win-win all the way across the board.

So how do you do this? You need a trusting relationship with the other lender, the other person who's going to bring their money in. They have to trust you because you have a track record. They have to know you well. They'll want to do some due diligence, maybe not the same level that you've done on your borrower, but they want some all the same.

In order to be transparent about why the other person should invest, you must be able to explain how private lending works. Explain it to them simply, yet in enough detail that they feel comfortable. Let them know that everything is done through an attorney and through a title company office. Explain the same thing that I've explained to you. It's safe because it's all done the way the big banks do it. We don't do it any differently on a small scale.

Typically, your connections do not need the same degree of experience, because they're relying on you. You've done the legwork, you explained to them how you do due diligence on the borrower, and the deal. They can even look over your shoulder, they're learning as they go. They also like the fact that in most cases, you put some of your own money in the deal. If it's just their money, then they may feel a little naked. If you have some of your money in the deal, they know that you're in with them. They know you will stand behind the deal, and if any problems do come up, you're the one who's in the position to talk to that borrower and mitigate any potential issues.

Your co-lenders will take a lesser yield or return on their money because they are not going to do all of the work you do, and they feel their time is more valuable doing other things. They just want to get their money in a safe place that's reliable, a place where they will earn a consistent and higher yield, and you're the one who can help them make that happen. You're offering them an opportunity to make more money, and a service that allows them passive income, without the research and details.

EXAMINE POTENTIAL ARBITRAGE PARTNER

Part of your research involves examining a potential arbitrage lender's background. You want to know their experience and preferences. Are they providing you with capital they have easy access to? Is it capital they would otherwise invest somewhere else, in the stock market or in a CD? Make sure it's not money they need to live on. (They shouldn't be looking for steady income, because you don't want to borrow money from someone who has to live on that money to buy daily essentials. You don't want that kind of responsibility on your back.) Are they familiar with real estate financing at all? It's better if they have some level of real estate experience because the less you have to explain to make them feel comfortable, the better. It doesn't mean you can't start with someone with less experience, but it takes more work to get them there.

Get a description from them about their comfortable range of investment. Do they have small accounts and IRAs they want to get started with, $5,000 or $10,000? Do they have $50,000 or $100,000, or do they have a lot more than that, but they want to do a few deals and see how it feels? Get an idea of where they stand on the amount of capital because then you can identify the right deals for your collaboration.

What kind of returns do they want? They need to be realistic. In the current market, it is totally adequate and reasonable for this passive partner to earn 6 percent to 8 percent. If they come to you and say, "Gee, I heard you can make double digits in real estate without lifting a finger," then you will need to educate them a little more. Somebody has to do some work, and if you're the one finding the access to the deals, and doing the due diligence, then the workload is one-sided. They don't deserve the same return. If they don't understand or appreciate that concept, they're not the right person for you.

Is this a person who, once they like what you're doing, is able to put more money into more deals? That would be a great person to work with because the fewer people you have to work with, the better. It just makes life simpler.

You also have to determine how long they're able to keep their capital invested. You don't want somebody who's putting their money out there and will need it back in three months to put their kids through college, pay property taxes, get their car fixed, or make a house repair. They have to be able to leave their money in for the duration of the deal, whether that's six months, twelve months, or three years.

Find out if they're willing to go outside their geographic area. What's their comfort zone? Are they willing to go to other markets besides their city or state that might be more suitable? If they are someone who wants to monitor the progress of a rehab, you need to know that up front.

What kind of asset is acceptable to them? We talked earlier about a single family being a great place to start. If you are more experienced and you're doing investing and private capital lending in apartments or commercial buildings and you want to go in that direction, that's fine. That requires a higher level of expertise and experience, so bear that in mind when you are vetting partners.

The right fit matters. Just as you have to make sure you have the right people on your team, and the right borrower, you also have to be diligent about knowing as much as you can about the people behind the money. They aren't just a means to an end. Don't see them simply as a supply of capital. The wrong lender partnership can make your life more difficult and can take some of the joy and passion out of your private lending business.

CHAPTER 17

UNDERSTANDING VALUE

I mentioned the investment to value ratio (ITV) in the last chapter. Let's take a closer look at it now that we are focusing on understanding the value of your deals. ITV is the total loan amount, divided by that property's total value after repairs. Let's take the same example from the last chapter: a property with an after-repaired value of $100,000 on which you agreed to loan the borrower a total of $75,000. That $75,000 incorporates both the acquisition cost and the additional money to renovate, for a total of $75,000. The investment to value ratio is 75 percent.

> ### Investment to Value (ITV)
> #### (Lender's Viewpoint)
>
> $100,000 = Property value, after repairs
> $75,000 = Investment to borrower, includes acquisition cost and renovation costs
> 75% = Investment to Value (ITV)
>
> #### Loan to Value (LTV)
> #### (Borrower's Viewpoint)
> Can be the same or different amount than ITV
> Typically 60% – 80%

It's critical when evaluating the ITV to know the property value. How do you ascertain that? You could research the property value and compare it to values of other similar properties. It's easy to gather this information online. You could also have a good realtor broker on your team who will give you comparable sale values on this area so you can see price-per-square-foot sales figures, and number of days on the market (activity level). That helps you ascertain the expected value of the property. Are you lending too much? You want that margin of safety, so ITV is critical.

Never rely on the word of the borrower or the owner of the property. They'll give you their assessment. That's fine to start with, but you still want a verifiable and trustworthy assessment. Do your due diligence, as we discussed earlier, and ascertain the facts so you feel totally comfortable with the amount of money you lend on that deal.

The loan to value ratio (LTV) is the investment from the borrower's standpoint. The loan to value can be the same as investment to value from the lender's standpoint, or they can be different.

Loan to value is calculated from the borrower's standpoint. If we're the borrower, we own the property, we're borrowing money from a private lender or the bank. We might want to borrow 80 percent of the value, which is typically what banks will do today for investors. That means the loan to value to the borrower is 80 percent. Why would the loan to value be different from the investment to value that you, as a private lender, might want to make? You might decide you'll loan 50 percent investment to value, which would be $50,000 on a $100,000 value property. The borrower might still need some extra money. He might go to somebody else in a secondary position and borrow an additional $30,000. The total loan to value for the borrower is 80 percent, but your investment value is only 50 percent. You have protected your first position. The borrower still got what he wanted, and his second lender is in second position, behind you on the title.

The upper recommended threshold for lending is typically

the range between 60 percent and 80 percent investment to value. How you look at it from your standpoint will depend on your risk tolerance and different aspects of the borrower and the actual collateral asset. If your investment to value starts to creep above 75 percent, 80 percent, closer to 85 percent, 90 percent, what you've done is increase your risk, because now there's very little margin at the top. The equity margin that you have above your investment is slim.

You're always looking at worst-case scenarios. They don't happen very often if you do your due diligence, but you always want a margin of safety. For instance, 5 percent to 10 percent of equity above your loan is typically not enough to cover the potential cost of collection. In the rare instance when you have to work through the collection foreclosure process, in some states it could take months. Now you are "upside down." You can no longer recoup your original principal, let alone your return on investment. Therefore, ITV is very important for you as a lender. The higher you go, the riskier the investment.

There are criteria for determining your investment to value ratio.

First, how well do you know the borrower? Have you done deals with him or her before? Do you have a track record? If it's your first time to do a deal with him, you might want to take less risk. Keep your investment to value down a little bit, down from 75 percent to maybe 65 percent or 60 percent, just to feel more comfortable. That's a prudent way to get started.

Geographic area and type of neighborhood. You know that due diligence incorporates the location of the property, the condition of the property, the neighborhood, and the activity level of sales in that neighborhood. Those are all key factors. If you want to invest in an area that is a bit less appealing, lower your ITV. If it looks like a rock-solid deal and you have a rock-solid borrower with a track record in an area with conforming properties, you might go as high as 75 percent or 80 percent.

The uniqueness of the property. You might find a non-conforming property that's cool because there's something different about it. It could be a slam dunk, but fewer people might find that property desirable because of its uniqueness. It could be unique based on the style of the home compared to the area, or it could be more rural than the rest of the local community. Those properties can make the investment riskier. In that case, lower your investment to value ratio.

Your limits and your geography. Realize that all real estate's local. There's a substantial difference between East Coast, West Coast, and Midwest markets. There can be national trends across the country, but every market has its own local economy. That's the inefficiency of the market. Another reason you might want to keep your ITV low is because although a particular market is volatile, you have a great borrower there who really has a lot of experience in that area. You keep the ITV low just to hedge your bets and protect yourself.

Be fully aware of your own financial comfort zone. If you're just getting started, stick to a lower ITV. If you have more experience, and a track record with the borrower, bump it up if you feel so inclined. You also need to decide if you put all your money into one property, or do you space it out. Do you segregate your investment allocations into different properties with different borrowers? Generally, we think it's good to be diversified. Plus, you get more experience that way. You're not putting everything on one property. If something happened to that one property, you don't want everything tied up there. You can also consider putting money on one big property, along with several smaller ones. Again, these are different ways for you to break up the basket of your investments. You have to look at all the factors together. There is no right or wrong; it's what fits your comfort zone. Just realize that these different variables that I've laid out are a big part of how you balance out your investment to value ratio and how you manage your capital.

As an investor, you want your capital fully invested. "Dead

money" is money that isn't working for you. The capital that you have available for investment that you don't need to maintain your lifestyle, should be working for you somewhere. If you decide it's in real estate, as a private capital lender, you'd like to have pretty close to 100 percent invested all the time. Here's the problem: money goes out for four, five, six, maybe eight or nine months on a shorter-term lending deal, after which you get paid off. When you get paid off, now you must go back to the market and find another investment deal. That takes some work. When the money comes back to you, sitting in your bank account at next to 0 percent, it's not earning squat. Even though you might, on a regular basis, get 10 percent or 11 percent or 12 percent on the returns from your borrower, if your money comes back and sits for two or three months at a time doing nothing, your overall yield starts to go down and even approaches high single digits.

There's nothing wrong with that; just realize what your returns really are. That's why I am going to explain longer-term lending, when you lend it out and forget it about it for a while. You get a regular return, which might be 8 percent or 9 percent or 10 percent. Overall, if you're getting low double digits, you're doing really well in this market, especially when you mitigate your risk.

Track your average time between deals. You may have a lot of short-term (six to twelve months) and midrange deals (two to three years). Do you have some longer-term deals that might even go five years or more? What's your overall average among those where you're keeping your money deployed? How hard do you have to work to keep that money deployed? How many deals are coming back to you where you have to redeploy the money with the same borrower or find another borrower who has an equally good track record and equally good opportunity?

A SHIFT IN THE MARKET

We know that markets cycle. Typically every six, seven, eight years there's a market cycle. Real estate goes through a cycle. Wall Street goes through a cycle. We know they exist. We don't pretend they don't. How do you hedge your bets, particularly as a private lender? One tool is the investment to value ratio. Some markets are more volatile than others. Some markets, when there's an upmarket, go up much more quickly and rise to a higher point, and then when there's a market reset, they drop faster.

If you're a private lender who loaned money on a deal that you thought was good, you did the due diligence and found a good borrower, you can still get caught in a downturn in the market. The key thing to remember about real estate is it doesn't drop like the stock market. It doesn't drop 20 percent, 30 percent in a week's time. The fastest we've ever seen real estate market drop has probably been in California where it dropped about 3 percent per month. You might say, "That's a big drop," but that's not the same as 30 percent in a week. There actually is time for you and the borrower to look at the market and say, "Wow, things have changed. We have to reset. The financial markets are turbulent right now. The credit markets are tightening up. The banks aren't lending money. People are tightening down. They're not buying. It looks like property values are going down. What do we do?"

There are a couple different options. You're dealing with real people, and that's another reason why it's such a great place to be in private lending. Real people are easier to deal with than banks, particularly when there's respect. Let's say the property value goes down, through no fault of your borrower. Or the contract on it fell through because the buyer couldn't get their financing and the market's tightened up. Now you have a conversation with your borrower. Is this property at a price point where they can rent it out for a couple years, so that you can get a decent return and you both can ride out the market until prices come back up? When the market goes down, it will come back up again. It takes some time, but that's one option.

Let's say you put a lot of money in, and that property's not going to rent for enough to get a good return for you. Then you have a different conversation with your borrower. "Look, maybe we just need to go ahead and sell, get what we can." Maybe both of you take a little bit of a hit on this one deal. You both cut your potential profits and maybe even put some money on the table to get rid of this property. It shouldn't be a lot. Percentage wise, you're probably not looking at very much money, but that's a decision that you have to look at and make accordingly.

If you stay in the price points where the after repair the value is $150,000 to $200,000, you'll be safe in nonvolatile markets. In those markets you can go to a plan B, rent the property out and hold it for a few years if you like. Just keep your finger on the pulse of the market. Watch what the markets are doing. Don't get greedy. When there's a chance to take your profit in a market that might be a little bit skittish, the best thing to do is take what you can and get out of the market quickly. Watch your ITV. Know what the markets look like. Stay in nonvolatile markets, and your chance of losing your money is very minimal.

Considering all the scenarios, calculate the total capital and collection costs that you believe you'd need to earn back if you have to take the property, foreclose it, repossess it, and sell it. What you come up with depends on the locale: it depends on the laws and regulations in that state. That's what you talk to the attorney about. If I'm investing in Arkansas, and I have to go through a foreclosure, what does that usually look like? What does the timeline look like? What if a borrower files for bankruptcy? Has that ever happened? Yes. Is it the worst case in the world? No, it's not. I've been through some borrowers' bankruptcies. It is not the worst thing in the world. There's a process. As a secured creditor, you have higher priority than other creditors to get to your collateral or get paid, one or the other. It will happen. Don't lose sleep over that.

The bankruptcies I've been involved in have not been by business owners. They've been owner occupants to whom I sold a house. That's where I've had my trouble. In private lending, we don't lend to owner occupants—consumers. We lend to business owners.

When you are deciding on your investment to value ratio, stay informed. Know how trustworthy the data are that you use to determine your investment to value. Did you get reliable information? Have you double-checked it? Have you cross referenced the comparable sale values (the after repaired value (ARV)) with two or three sources, your own internet research, a realtor or licensed agent, broker, and management people? Have you ascertained from different people if the number you have is a good value for this property? Make sure the data being used are current data with accurate sources. Once you know a market area and you've been doing deals there, then you are better informed. Until you know the market, double- and triple-check.

CHAPTER 18

THE STRUCTURE OF A DEAL

Let's focus on how your deals will be structured. There are key elements that make up each deal. Consider each of them up front before you hand your money to any borrower.

Structure of a Deal

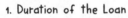

1. Duration of the Loan
2. Active Involvement
3. Passive Involvement
4. Dodd-Frank Law
5. Rates of Return
6. Borrower's Hard Money
7. Dealing with Defaulted Borrower

DURATION OF THE LOAN

The duration of the loan term is driven by whether you are going to be more active or passive as an investor. Short term will be typically less than twelve months. Shorter-term loans are regarded as being more active: money in, money out, money in, money out.

Midterm loans run from one year up to three or five years. A longer-term loan is anything more than five years. The longer your money is in a deal, the more passive your activity. It's out there, fully deployed, and you are not having to find new deals for it soon.

ACTIVE INVOLVEMENT

The benefit of being actively involved in shorter-term investments of twelve months or less is in the velocity of money. Velocity of money is a measure of how often you "turn" an amount of capital from one deal to the next. That takes active work. Your rate of return is potentially going to be higher with short-term loans, but your ability to keep your money working at that rate becomes difficult the more money you have to invest.

If it's a small amount of money it's feasible to turn that money more frequently. The more capital you have to invest, the harder it is to keep all that money turning frequently. For example, if you have several million dollars and you want to keep it all in shorter-term loans, that's a lot of work because you have to be in and out of deals all the time. Almost every week you'll be talking to borrowers, and attorneys, and title companies.

If that's what you like to do and you want to work your money, that's a great way to do it. If you want more passive and you're happy with less work and a little bit lower return, then longer term makes more sense.

Active involvement requires more time and more communication with the borrower and all the other parties on your team. You have to keep tabs on all of the projects. Being very active is often correlated to creating a business from this activity.

In other words, it's more business investment than a passive investment. It demands far more time for you to manage your accounts.

PASSIVE INVOLVEMENT

Passive involvement, on the other hand, refers to deals consisting of those mid- or longer-term loans. It's often favored by those who want less effort or stress, people who may once have owned or run a business but don't want to run one anymore.

Passive is more often referred to as "set it and forget it." You get payments on a regular basis so you know the money's well invested, but you don't have to be involved with the ins and outs of the project. After careful due diligence, you let those checks roll in month after month.

Passive involvement requires fewer follow-ups with fewer inspections and project timelines after you do your initial due diligence. It will reduce your workload, minimize your effort with repeated due diligence in between projects, and it offers you more time to find the next lending deal. Less stress, less work, all the way around.

DODD-FRANK LAW

You might hear people in real estate and investment talk about Dodd-Frank. This law was created after the last recession, the financial downturn of 2008 to 2010, and what followed. Senator Chris Dodd and Congressman Barney Frank wrote the law, also known as the Consumer Financial Protection Act. A government bureau called the Consumer Financial Protection Bureau governs it.

In response to the 2008 financial market and housing crash, the Dodd-Frank Law put controls on the financial marketplace that affect everything in Wall Street and banking. It also affects our ability to make certain types of loans, even as private capital investors. Even though we're not regulated like banks, there are some relevant regulations here.

Specific laws determine how loans may be issued and to whom. Dodd-Frank also regulates private lenders who lend to consumers. "Consumer" in this case in real estate is a homeowner or owner occupant. But remember the distinction we made earlier in this section that as a private lender, you lend to business people who don't live in the home. They are not the occupants; they fix up the houses to rent or resell. That's the big difference. Loaning to consumers can become very complex. There are too many regulations and licenses to do direct consumer lending. There are far fewer regulations for lending to business owners or investors.

The Dodd-Frank Law does not apply to nonowner occupied residential property or commercial property. If it's not owner occupied, it's called commercial property. In that case, this law does not apply, and that's the good news.

RATES OF RETURN

Various factors affect the rates of return. The first is to identify the class of asset. In other words, you have our favorite, the single-family houses, which is the best place for you to get started because it's easy to evaluate and it has a lower price point.

Commercial property and unique properties are a different ball game altogether. If you wanted to move up the ladder to that kind of lending, that's your choice, but don't start there. Single family is far easier and has less risk than the other asset classes. Unique properties may have a higher potential reward or return, but they have much higher risk. Unique is another code word for risk—keep that in mind.

A typical or median rate of return today for short-term lending is 10 percent to 12 percent. You might consider a lower return if the property you're investing in is in a really good, safe neighborhood, if you have a very experienced borrower with a strong track record, and if the amount of rehab or renovation being undertaken is relatively minimal. All those factors reduce your risk. If your real risk is reduced, then it probably makes sense for you not to go for the higher return. There's a balance to be found, so consider that when you're looking at your rates of return. You might, on the other hand, want to charge a higher rate of return if the property you're investing in or loaning money against has a higher price point than your usual deal.

In the marketplace today, anything above $150,000 is risky. If we decide to do a deal above that, we'll ask for a higher rate of return because our risk is higher. If the property is unique or requires more work, it may take longer to sell, resulting in our having to be in the deal longer, which again increases our risk. Also, if your borrower is less experienced, has a shorter track record or no track record at all, then you definitely can negotiate a higher rate of return to help offset some of the risk you're taking.

BORROWER'S "HARD MONEY"

Hard money is what is actually paid into a project by the borrower. If there's a little bit more risk, we may ask the borrower to put some of his or her own money in the deal. Let's say the borrower requests $75,000 to do the acquisition and rehab, and he wants 100 percent of that $75,000 from us. If we feel like there's more risk in this deal, we may ask him to put $15,000 of his own money in the deal, meaning we lend $60,000 instead of the $75,000. Having his own hard money in their own deal minimizes our risk and puts him more at risk. This is a great motivator to keep the project moving and successful for both parties. The borrower has skin in the game. Sure, they have time and effort—but let's say they have their own hard money in this deal and they don't have hard money in another deal. Which investment property do you think they'll give more attention to? They become more invested in your project because they want to get their money out, just like you want to get your money out. You have more assurance of the deal's success.

You could also combine multiple draws on the loan with borrower hard money. Here's what that looks like. The borrower puts his or her money into the deal to start the rehab, but they need money from you to complete. They are investing their money in the deal and then taking draws on a scheduled basis, contingent on passing inspections. Again, this reduces the risk so your money's not all in the deal at once. You know the property's being rehabbed on schedule, which minimizes your potential downside if other things happen.

You might also require hard money from a borrower if he or she is less familiar to you, or if he or she has an uncertain or short track record rehabbing properties. Maybe the property value or loan amounts are higher than your normal deals, or the project is more unique, which carries a higher risk in itself.

DEALING WITH A DEFAULTED BORROWER

Let's say your borrower's payments have been coming in, and then all of a sudden they go dark. They stop communicating. I described a worst case with a natural disaster or negligence or casualty on the property. That will be covered by insurance, but what about a borrower who has something happen to him? He gets sick, maybe passes away. A family member gets sick. There's a divorce. There's a drug issue. All kinds of things can happen in life with the best people, so think about the worst case and be prepared to initiate collections. The payments stop. Your remedy, the default terms, are in the promissory note. That promissory note is the contract that your attorney drew up when you made the deal to lend the money.

The interest rate, the term, when the payments are to be made—all those aspects are in that contract. The borrower is now in default because they're not making payments. As the lender you have the legal position securing your investment in the property, a first lien position. It gives you a priority control over the property if the borrower is in default.

Here are the actions you can take. Your attorney can initiate a collection process right away, and we recommend that. Any time a borrower is late more than five days on scheduled payments, we initiate communication with the borrower and go to the attorney to begin collection. They still have time to make it up, so doing this doesn't mean you'll foreclose; it simply starts the foreclosure timeline. The borrower is informed that he or she is in default, has X number of days to pay, and a foreclosure will commence on a specific date.

Your attorney will do this because he or she knows how to handle this correctly. Each state has its own particular rules and regulations on collections and foreclosure, so be sure to use an attorney who's in the state where your property is located.

Let's say the worst-case scenario happens and you end up

with the property. Your attorney has taken the collection all the way through foreclosure and now gives you the deed. You are now no longer the bank; you are now the proud owner of a property you didn't want. If you've set your investment to value ratio at the right level (no more than 75 percent), the likelihood of you being able to wholesale (offer that property for sale to another investor), and still get your money back AND make a profit, is pretty high.

Calculate the entire amount you want to recoup from the property. That would include your entire principal of your loan amount, collection fees that the attorney will charge, foreclosure fees, the loan servicer fees, any outstanding taxes, and the extra staffing costs involving administration of this collection.

As the current owner of the property, you may have some property taxes, insurance and maybe even some utility costs from maintaining the property for a short period of time until you resell it. You also want at least a small profit. All of these fees are why you stick to no more than a 75 percent investment to value. The remaining 25 percent margin is what you'll need to cover your fees and profit.

If you do your due diligence and structure your deal right, you can still make money if the deal goes sideways. This rarely happens, but if and when it does, mitigate your risk of taking a loss on an investment. That's still a much better deal than "playing" the stock market or waiting for your measly .01 percent interest on your money from your bank. Don't let one bad deal taint your private lending experience. It's happened to all of us and not only have we survived it, we've learned a hell of a lot from it and continue to love private lending.

CHAPTER 19

PRACTICES OF THE DEAL

Now it's time to get down to the more intricate ways of lending your money. It all starts with the term sheet.

This is a simple document, typically one page that clearly outlines the deal. It's the initial document between the lender and borrower. It's the essence of the deal: it defines in writing what was agreed to verbally. It outlines in summary form the terms and conditions. It's critical that any important term is clearly and precisely listed in this term sheet. It is given to the attorney who will write the rest of the documents from the term sheet.

ELEMENTS OF THE TERM SHEET

It all starts with the basics and goes into more specifics from there.

- Property and address
- Total loan amount
- Investment to value
- Terms of repayment (when will payments be made)
- Maturity date of the loan (six months, twelve months, three years, etc.)
- Payments are principal and interest, or interest only
- Possible extensions you might be willing to offer under certain conditions
- Acquisition costs—how much the borrower is planning to pay for the property per the contract
- Estimated and agreed-upon time frames for renovations
- Determines if there will be a loan servicer
- Legal fees and other fees paid by the borrower for settling the documentation of the loan
- Draw schedule
- Example: three draws in equal payments over three months
- The rate of return (interest rate)
- Schedule for performing inspections
- Agreed-upon fees for inspections (by licensed inspector or contractor)
- Extension terms in the event the property does not sell on time

All of these items are negotiable and they all need to be included in your term sheet.

DEBT INSTRUMENT

The debt instrument or promissory note is the contract that you use to create your private lending investment. The debt instrument is the most common way that loans are made. That's typically how you borrow money to buy any kind of property. When you have a debt instrument, the principal is paid back over a certain period of time, plus interest. Payments are scheduled over an agreed-upon period of time, per the promissory note contract.

EQUITY BASIS DEAL

In an equity basis lending deal, instead of earning interest, you get a percentage of the net profit paid back to you, in addition to the original principal invested. Instead of stated interest, there could be a profit percentage negotiated into this instrument. This agreement can be more complex. It requires greater definition but can be good for both the borrower and the lender. An example of when an equity basis deal would make sense would be at a higher price-point property. Let's say you have a good borrower who has a good track record. He or she is into a higher price-point property. They do good work. You know they have good contractors, so you are willing to take a little bit more risk.

As the lender, you can potentially make a higher rate of return by taking a percentage of the profit, but it's not guaranteed. From the borrower's standpoint, this kind of deal can be a safeguard because there are no regular interest payments to make during the life of this loan. Everyone waits until the property is sold. Then the borrower gives you part of the profit. It could be a good deal, but you need to weigh the pros and cons between your risk tolerance and profit, and also what's good for your borrower.

An equity basis deal requires you to do additional due diligence to understand the full scope of the deal and its risks. A higher-price point property, a more involved type of renovation, will take longer. The current and soon-to-be marketplace, as well as the uniqueness of the property, are also factors that can add risk to the deal. If you're adding risk, you need to charge a higher interest rate, or you can do a profit share deal where your potential return could be very good, better than a debt instrument. On the other hand, if the profit margin is smaller or next to nothing, you may come away with very little. It's a little bit of a risk you have to take in exchange for a greater potential for higher profit.

For a typical equity basis deal, the lender might receive 33 percent of the net profit on the sale of the property. It could be 25 percent. It could be 50 percent, but 33 percent is an average. The borrower gives up potentially a higher profit, but avoids paying interest. If it takes longer to sell the property, that doesn't cost the borrower more money. It doesn't take more of their cash flow revenues out of their operations.

Stay away from equity basis deals unless you're more experienced. The market research done by both you and the borrower is critical to determining the likelihood of selling a property in a certain time frame. That's also why you stay away from unique properties if at all possible. It's just hard to determine what that exit plan will be. The potential profits can be notably higher than charging a fixed interest rate over a twelve-month period, but they also can be less if the profit sharing plan doesn't work out.

HYBRID DEALS

You can also create an either-or agreement, such as a hybrid deal. As a lender you can put a stated amount of interest, let's say 8 percent or the greater of 33 percent of the net profits. Now you've hedged your bets. You will at least get 8 percent, but if the deal works out really well for the borrower, and it's a little bit higher price-point deal and a little bit more risk, then you can also get a higher return at 33 percent. If the deal doesn't work out great for the borrower, you get your 8 percent, which is a still a good return (remember, it's more than eight times what your bank is offering).

The hybrid deal is an extra safety platform for you as the lender and gives you the best of both worlds. Base most of the deals you do on the debt instrument because that's the conventional way, especially when you're getting started.

As you become more experienced, you can venture into equity basis and hybrids.

CONVERTIBLE DEBT INSTRUMENT

The convertible debt instrument is a debt instrument that can convert or be changed to another type, such as an equity or a profit share deal. Generally the decision to convert occurs after the project has been started. The actual instrument itself is negotiated and put into place by your attorney before you lend any money. This agreement is defined and spelled out in the contract or the promissory note before the parties agree.

For example, you might have your typical 12 percent interest rate on a six- or twelve-month deal. The deal can be written so that, at your sole discretion, you have the opportunity to convert to a profit percentage or an equity deal if you want. That puts all the balls in your court, doesn't it? It lets you have at least your interest rate if you want that, but if you see this deal is really working out well, the market is really hot, and there's going to be a great profit, you can convert the deal and take the profit percentage.

Don't convert to profit unless there's a lot of profit. If there is, everybody gets something. If you're the lender, and you're doing a higher price-point deal, this might be an opportunity for you to seek higher profits than available through the regular debt instrument. Everything is up for negotiation. You won't do this on every deal, but certain deals might lend themselves well to a convertible debt instrument. Remember, it begins as a standard debt instrument, and the principal plus interest is still paid back, as on a standard debt instrument deal.

Here's how the conversion happens. At your option (as the lender) you can switch the deal anytime to an equity agreement with notification to the borrower. Conversion to an equity basis might not always be in the borrower's best interest. It may take more of his or her profit, but if there's a lot of profit, if the pie is bigger, everybody gets a little bit bigger piece. They'll still do well. Everyone makes good money and because you set up the concept of a convertible debt instrument at the beginning, it will not come as a surprise to the borrower.

CHAPTER 20

DOCUMENTS AND PAYMENTS

I've described some of the documents you'll work with. Here I'll go through all of them in more detail, and add a few more to the list.

PROMISSORY NOTE

This is exactly what it sounds like; it's the promise—a contract—to pay back the loan. It's what your borrower will sign as the debt instrument. The attorney draws it up and it stipulates the amount of money you're loaning, the interest rate, how the money will be paid back, when the money has to be paid back (the maturity date). It's also known as the Note Payable. This promissory note describes the lending agreement between the borrower and the lender. It usually is not recorded in public records, although it can be.

SECURITY AGREEMENT

In about half the states, the security agreement is known as a mortgage. In the rest it's called a Deed of Trust. The only difference between the two is that some states use what's called a "judicial foreclosure process," which means foreclosure proceedings have to go through the courts. That happens in the mortgage states. In the Deed of Trust states, foreclosure is a little bit faster and does not have to go through the court system. The security agreement is always recorded in the public record. That's what gives you, the lender, what we call a "perfected lien" against the property. It puts you in the chain of title. The public's on notice that you have loaned money against this property and no one else can sell the property without paying you off. It gives you recorded evidence of title.

TERM SHEET

The term sheet, as I explained in the last chapter, is a simple, typically one-page agreement written between you and your borrower. The attorney does not have to write it. You can give this to the attorney, who uses it as the road map to create the lending documents.

The term sheet memorializes all the agreed-upon details of the deal, specifies the property, describes the loan amount, the payment, the interest rate, and any fees involved. It will also describe the rehab, what level of rehabs can be done, what the schedule of rehabs will be, any inspections, time frames, and any extension terms that you might wish to negotiate with your borrower.

INSURANCE POLICY

The insurance policy will cover the property for any damage—natural, negligent, or otherwise—and gives you, as the lender, what you need to protect your interest in the property. It also provides protection if the borrower allows his own policies to lapse.

ADDITIONAL DOCUMENTS

Two items we have not discussed are the closing statement and title policy, both handled by the closing title office or attorney escrow.

CLOSING STATEMENT

The closing statement is what the title company uses to lay out the loan amounts, the total cost, acquisition cost, any fees involved with closing, recording, recording attorney fees, and any taxes that need to be paid. It discloses what amounts have been paid, and by whom. It documents the entire transaction. Both the lender and borrower sign. It's good for your records, it establishes a cost basis for the borrower, and everything's laid out there in black and white.

TITLE POLICY

The title policy is very important, as it insures title. There are two different types of policies. In an owner's title policy, the borrower (the buyer), gets a title policy that insures the title for that owner. You, the lender, also get a policy that insures your position in the title as far as a lender. If you're loaning "x" amount of money, and you'll be in a first lien position, which is the safest, most secure position, that title policy will dictate you have a first lien position. If you're lending in a secondary position, it will dictate that. If there's ever a claim against the property, you as the lender, and also the owner of the property, will be made whole by these policies, which insure the title.

STAGING YOUR LOAN PAYOUTS/DRAWS

Often you don't want to provide all the money for the acquisition and rehab all at once. You might provide funds for the acquisition and the first portion of rehab at closing, and then stage out the remainder of the rehab funds (draws) on a draw schedule. The draw schedules are typically determined by the wholesale joint venture partner as part of their renovation schedule. They'll have a schedule that states, "I'm going to do so much in this week, and so much here, and so much here." They'll lay it out in two, three, or four different schedules, depending upon the duration of the rehab and how involved it is. That will be the schedule by which you'll pay.

When they say, "We've completed phase number one," you send your contractor or inspector over, they document it, and if phase one's been completed, you wire the funds for the completion of that phase. It's all laid out in advance. It's wise to pay out a sizable rehab project in at least two or three segments. A $10,000 rehab may be broken into two equal segments. Rehabs of more than $10,000 are usually broken into three or more segments. Use more segments for tighter control, according to your comfort level, your track record, and your experience level. The more draws you have, of course, the more work is involved, but the tighter your controls are on the entire rehab.

Each draw is given out after the prior stage passes inspection. Use that local inspector or contractor on your team, who will be paid by the borrower for that inspection on your behalf. Additional inspections help keep tabs on the project quality, reduce the risk of your invested capital being put in the deal too quickly, and prevent the borrower from using your money for something else instead. You don't have to go back to the title company. You've already established the documents for the loan, which has been laid out and fully documented. Now, it's just between you and the borrower. You can wire directly to their account upon sign-off by your inspector that the rehab phase has been completed.

Some borrowers don't like draws. They take more time. Not that they're trying to commit fraud, but they just like to roll. They like to have all the money in their account so they can go as fast as possible. It's not a bad thing, but it doesn't protect you. Remember, we live by the concept of "trust but verify." Imagine your borrower pushes back and says, "Look, I'm getting this project done in two weeks." Well, what if they don't? What if something happens and now you've given them all the money, and they've used it for something else or even a different project? Break draws into phases to protect yourself.

The borrower can sometimes get pushy. When you're first getting started, we highly recommend you do a multiple draw schedule so you understand how it works. The borrower may say they can work faster without draws; it's easier without draws, but draws give you more control over the success of the project and protects your investment.

LEGAL COMPONENTS OF CLOSING THE TRANSACTION

Remember, you need an attorney who is located in the same state as the property and the title company because they know the rules for lending and real estate transactions in that state. They will draft your documents from your term sheet, verify all of your interests are being met and requests complied with. The title company is that third party that holds your funds until all of the criteria for your lending have been laid out. Your attorney will give them specific directions. Do not release your funds until all documents have been executed, until a fire insurance policy has been provided, and until the title policy is in place. The title company cannot release funds until that checklist has been completed.

The title company, through the title policy, will confirm that the title is clear for both the owner and you, the lender. Sometimes there are family inheritance issues, and the seller has to get a number of different parties to sign off their interest in order to sell the property. A title company makes sure that all claims, judgments, or encumbrances are settled. That protects your lien position.

The attorney can also verify that the title policy doesn't have any exclusions that would impair your title or your position in that property. The title company or the escrow agent will handle the remainder of all the legal activities. They make sure all of the documents are properly executed and notarized. They'll record executed documents that need to be recorded in the public records. They will send originals to the parties, which the originals need to go to. They'll send the title policy to the lender and a title policy to the owner. They'll send verification that insurance endorsement is in place to you. And they may also assist with setting up the borrower with a loan servicer, who is sometimes used to assist with processing loan payments.

CHAPTER 21

LOAN SERVICES, GUARANTEES, AND CAVEATS

Wow, congratulations! You've made it to the final chapter and you're about to embark on a wonderful adventure into passive income through real estate. I am so excited for you to experience the thrill of the deal and the ease of private lending rates of return. After you're finished, I promise you'll wonder why you ever settled for what the banks and your stocks portfolio were earning you. It's all massive success from here. But first, it's time to get through a few more technical loan details: what the loan servicer does, information about personal guarantees, and the final look at managing caveats.

LOAN SERVICER

A loan servicer is a licensed third-party company. They help manage the loan and its activities. A loan servicer does a variety of tasks for private lenders, whereas banks have their own servicing companies for their loans. A loan servicer will handle and process all the borrower's payments. They keep track of the payments and the date that they come in. If there's a late fee, they assess that. If you have an amortizing loan, meaning the loan is paying both interest and principal, they'll keep track of the loan balance for you.

We love using loan servicers. Sure, you could get the software and do some of the accounting and bookkeeping we talked about, but we recommend you outsource it. When you're first getting started, it's okay to manage a lot of your own details. You don't necessarily need a loan servicer for six- to twelve-month deals, because those are relatively short. Short-term tracking is relatively straightforward and uncomplicated for the private lender. When you start doing midrange to longer term, it's nice to have a loan servicer in place.

The cost for loan servicing is approximately $20 a month plus a $75 to $100 initial setup fee. Realize that your borrower pays for the loan services, a cost that is identified in the term sheet and not a cost to you.

ESCROW

Escrow is also called an impound account. It exists to hold funds in reserve for payment of property taxes and insurance when those bills are due. Property taxes and insurance are typically due on an annual basis, depending upon where a property is located and when the insurance policy was originated. You don't want to have a borrower who is unable to budget very well come up to a date when a property tax bill is due or insurance policy premium is due, and all of a sudden they're short of money. To offset that risk, a loan servicer will collect approximately 1/12th of the estimated total insurance and property bill each month. They keep that in an escrow account. Now the borrower doesn't have to come up with money when the premium comes due for taxes or insurance. The loan servicer gets that bill and they pay it.

The servicer also manages the loan balance so everybody knows exactly what the loan balance is at any time. When there's a payoff, the loan servicer provides that payoff amount to the closing agent.

IRS COMPLIANCE

Another nice part of loan servicing is that the servicer will take care of all the IRS compliance issues. The IRS requires that certain annual documents are provided to both lenders and borrowers. The loan servicer will handle those documents on your behalf. Also, they'll help you with a collection account if a borrower goes into default or is late on a payment. You can go right to your servicer because they already have the legal compliance in place. They can start collection letters. They can even help you with foreclosure and have a legal team for that purpose.

INSURANCE POLICIES

The insurance premium bill will be sent to the loan servicer so it is paid and renewed at the proper time. The servicer will always get your authorization to pay these premiums.

LOAN GUARANTEES

This is an important concept because a lot of your business loans to your investors will be done through entities (LLC, S-corporation, or corporations) that their attorneys or CPAs recommended they set up. The thing you need to realize as a private lender is that if they're doing business through an entity and signing off as an officer or a manager of that entity, then the entity is what stands behind that loan, in addition to your property collateral.

This is why you should know about personal guarantees, why they might be a good idea and when to use them.

When a person individually signs a promise to pay back a

debt, they are basically saying the property stands as collateral and, if the property is not enough, then their personal assets are on the line, too. Those are the terms of what we call a full recourse loan. If they sign through a corporate entity as a manager, officer, or agent, they're not signing individually. Only the assets of that company or that entity stand behind the loan (plus the collateral property that you're loaning on and which always is there for you). When a representative of a corporate entity signs a contract, only the business can be pursued for any defaults in which the property collateral is not sufficient to provide the money owed to you as the lender. The individual person is not liable for default. You can't pursue compensation from him or her.

When the borrower is contracting and doing business and signing loan documents through the business, then you might want to consider getting a personal guarantee. It is standard practice for banks to require a personal guarantee. Anytime I did any business with a bank (which has been rare), they always made me sign both as an officer of the company and give my personal guarantee. It's what I call a belts and suspenders approach. Banks always want it—why shouldn't you? If you're lending to a new borrower, somebody you don't have a track record with, especially if you are a new lender, go ahead and ask for that personal guarantee.

If the person is doing business as an entity, just add the

borrower's individual or personal guarantee. Your attorney will take care of the rest for you. The guarantee can be done on the same documents. There is a place on the promissory note and the security agreement for the officer of the entity to sign as an officer; right below, they can also sign as an individual. Sometimes two documents are used, one for the business and one for the individual. Your attorney can decide what the best practices are for that particular state.

The personal guarantee gives you an additional means to recoup a potential loss. You might not always be able to sell the property to recoup your loss if you're in a volatile state, or if your investment to value is too high, or if you're investing in a riskier deal. Normally, with good due diligence, you're looking at the collateral property as your primary backup if things go bad. In the case where the property value might be less than your principal, with a personal guarantee you do have the right to collect a deficiency (a judgment) against the individual. If a business is the only one guaranteeing the note and the business goes defunct, then you only have the assets of the business (if there is anything left).

In the world of the people we do business with, it's very unlikely that we would resort to a personal lawsuit because we've done our due diligence, and we've kept our investment to value ratio correct. Use a personal guarantee if you feel more comfortable with it. Your attorney can advise you and help you create best practices.

CAVEATS IN PRIVATE LENDING

In every business, every industry, there are always fraud-sters and scammers. They'll be out there to take advantage of your propensity to do business. We've probably all been manipulated at some point in our lives to do something we later regretted because we trusted somebody. We didn't verify.

In other cases there are people who don't intentionally mislead, they just don't have good business practices or they make mistakes. They don't have good operations. The problem may not be fraud, it just may be negligence. Either way, you have to protect yourself. Always document, document, document. Have your attorneys and your team make sure every I is dotted and every T is crossed. Sometimes people don't have the experience to successfully complete a deal. They're just getting involved, rehabbing properties in the marketplace, and are going through a learning curve. Maybe they don't know how to deal with subcontractors. Maybe they don't pay their contractors on time. Always use your due diligence as a first and principal defense against these kinds of people.

Random life events can kill a deal—things that happen to good people that can make a deal go south. What's your worst-case scenario? It could be unforeseen financial issues, health problems, unknown or misinterpreted regulations, construction or planning problems, or zoning problems. If everybody did as they promised or intended to do, there would never be issues, but that's not life. We have to realize that with everything we do in life, if we want a better success record, if we want a chance for a higher return on profit, we have to take some risk. Life and investing are the same way. You have to take a little bit of risk, so mitigate that risk.

Always, always do your due diligence on the people, the actual property project, and the geographic marketplace. Have experienced team members in place who help you do the due diligence, and help you track a process and a project. Make sure your attorney is on top of all the documents. Make sure your attorney is in the right state and very familiar with the local statutes and regulations. Verify that a borrower is not borrowing from local people for the same project. How do you do that? You go through a title company. They will insure your title, so if there is a fraudster or a scammer out there and they try to pull that, the title insurance will back you up. They'll verify. They will cover you if someone tries to pull that so you're not at risk.

The final check is for you to get your lender's title policy. If somebody pulls something off and there's a claim against your property, you will be paid off, and your borrower will be paid out. Everybody's happy. Remember, stay away from projects that are beyond the scope of your experience. You're just getting started. Don't dig in too deep. There are always opportunities in the marketplace for you to do safe deals. Start with experienced borrowers on easy projects, not extensive projects.

Stick with your price points on a project. You might decide you don't want to go above investing $75,000 or $80,000 in any one deal. Stick with that. Wait until you find that right deal for you. Don't stretch until you're ready to stretch. Starting with smaller deals is really smart. Don't jump into those big ones right away. Stay away from trying to hit home runs. Hitting those base hits over and over and over again provides a steady return and gets your principal back. So long as you don't get involved with the wrong borrowers on the wrong projects, you won't burn out and you'll love to stay in this private lending arena. It's about investing, not gambling.

Don't get greedy and unrealistic by demanding an excessively high interest rate. It's much better to work on a rate of return that gives a good margin of safety to your borrower so that they make a profit and will come back and do more business with you. If the market deems the interest rate should be dropped, to stay in business with that person, drop your interest rate a little bit. Sometimes rates go down; they fluctuate with the market. Know what the market is. Get a feel for that. Stay online with the forums. See what the word is on the street for current interest rates. Be sure to match your interest rates, your draws, and your hard money to the risk level of the project.

Find your mentors. There are always people out in the space who love to give back. Find those people. Take them out to lunch or dinner or buy them coffee. Their experience can be invaluable for you when you're getting started. It's fantastic to find someone in your marketplace who can look over your shoulder and answer questions. You're already on your way after having read this book. Learn from the best. Learn from the experts. That's what saves you more time than anything at all.

Now that you've made it to this final point, I have free resources for you available at KentClothier.com/BookResources. These include videos on how to become a private lender, as well as an opportunity to go through our academy and learn directly from one of the best instructors in the country on private lending. We've prepared a certification course that will walk you through step-by-step-by-step on how to set up a private lending situation for you. You can easily go right there and get signed up.

FINAL THOUGHTS

I've illustrated three situations for you, all of them passive, some more passive than others. But I completely understand there are many of you that believe even this is not passive enough. I'm excited to tell you that we have a really special opportunity to work directly with us. We recently went through an incredibly arduous process to get approved by the SCC and FINRA to start a Reg A investment fund.

But the point of this fund is to help investors that simply don't want to do wholesaling, don't necessarily want to be a private lender, and don't necessarily want to buy rental income. They want all the benefits of passive income with real estate, but they want to be even more hands-off. They want it done inside of their self-directed IRA or self-directed 401(k). If that's you, then I invite you to go to InvestWithKent.com. We will arrange to get you more information about the fund, and have a private consultation with you about how we can best serve you.

ACKNOWLEDGMENTS

To my family that has always shown me unrelenting support and motivation to keep moving forward and becoming the best version of myself. Your support is everything.

ABOUT THE AUTHOR

KENT CLOTHIER is the CEO of Real Estate Worldwide, a software training company for real estate investors, and the founder of the Boardroom Mastermind, the most elite real estate investor networking group in the country. He's flipped thousands of homes over the past fifteen years and helped tens of thousands of people learn how to do the same. He is passionate about teaching what he's learned in a simple way so that it's easy for anyone to connect the dots. As a husband and the proud father of three amazing kids, Kent has built the ultimate life for himself and his family.